234

Death Certificate

OFFICE OF THE COUNTY MEDICAL EXAMINER
858 Madison Avenue
MEMPHIS, TENNESSEE 38103

REPORT OF INVESTIGATION BY COUNTY MEDICAL EXAMINER

DECEDENT: Elvis Aron Presley RACE: W SEX: M AGE: 42

HOME ADDRESS: 3764 Elvis Presley Blvd M W S D OCCUPATION: Entertainer

TYPE OF DEATH (Check one only): Violent ☐ Casualty ☐ Suicide ☐ Suddenly when in apparent health ☐ Found Dead ☒
In Prison ☐ Suspicious, unusual or unnatural ☐ Cremation ☐

Comment _____
If Motor Vehicle Accident Check One: Driver ☐ Passenger ☐ Pedestrian ☐ Unknown ☐
Notification by: City Homicide Address: City
Investigating Agency: SCME + MPD

DESCRIPTION OF BODY: Clothed ☐ Unclothed ☒ Partly Clothed ☐ Circumcised Yes ☐ No ☐
Eyes: Bl Hair: Bl Mustache: — Beard: —
Weight: ___ Pounds Length: ___ Inches Body Temp: ___ Fahrenheit Date: ___
Rigor: Yes ☒ No ☐ Lyvor ___ Color ___ Fixed ☐ Non-Fixed ☐

Marks and Wounds:

Congestion of lungs
...

Autopsy at BMH

CANCELLED

PROBABLE CAUSE OF DEATH	MANNER OF DEATH	DISPOSITION OF CASE

HCVD associated with ASHD	(Check one only)
	Accident ☐ Natural ☒
	Suicide ☐ Unknown ☐
	Homicide ☐ Pending ☐
		1. Not a medical examiner case ☐
		2. Autopsy requested Yes ☐ No ☐
		   Autopsy ordered Yes ☐ No ☐
		   Pathologist _____

I hereby declare that after receiving notice of the death described herein I took charge of the body and made inquiries regarding the cause of death in accordance with Section 38-701-38-714 Tennessee Code Annotated; and that the information contained herein regarding such death is true and correct to the best of my knowledge and belief.

Date: 10/21/77 County of Appointment: _____ Signature of County Medical Examiner: _____

Revised 2-1-67
CME-1

WANTED ALIVE!

World's GREATEST Entertainer!!!

ELVIS AARON PRESLEY

REWARD
£2 MILLION!!!

For details, see Page 96

The ELVIS SPOTTERS Guide

Nic van Oudtshoorn

"All the actors I met in Hollywood told me that dying was a big moment, a big scene for anybody in the game. They told me it was a hard thing to do. So I did it. I think it came off pretty good but I'll be waiting to see how the experts feel about that."

- Elvis Aaron Presley

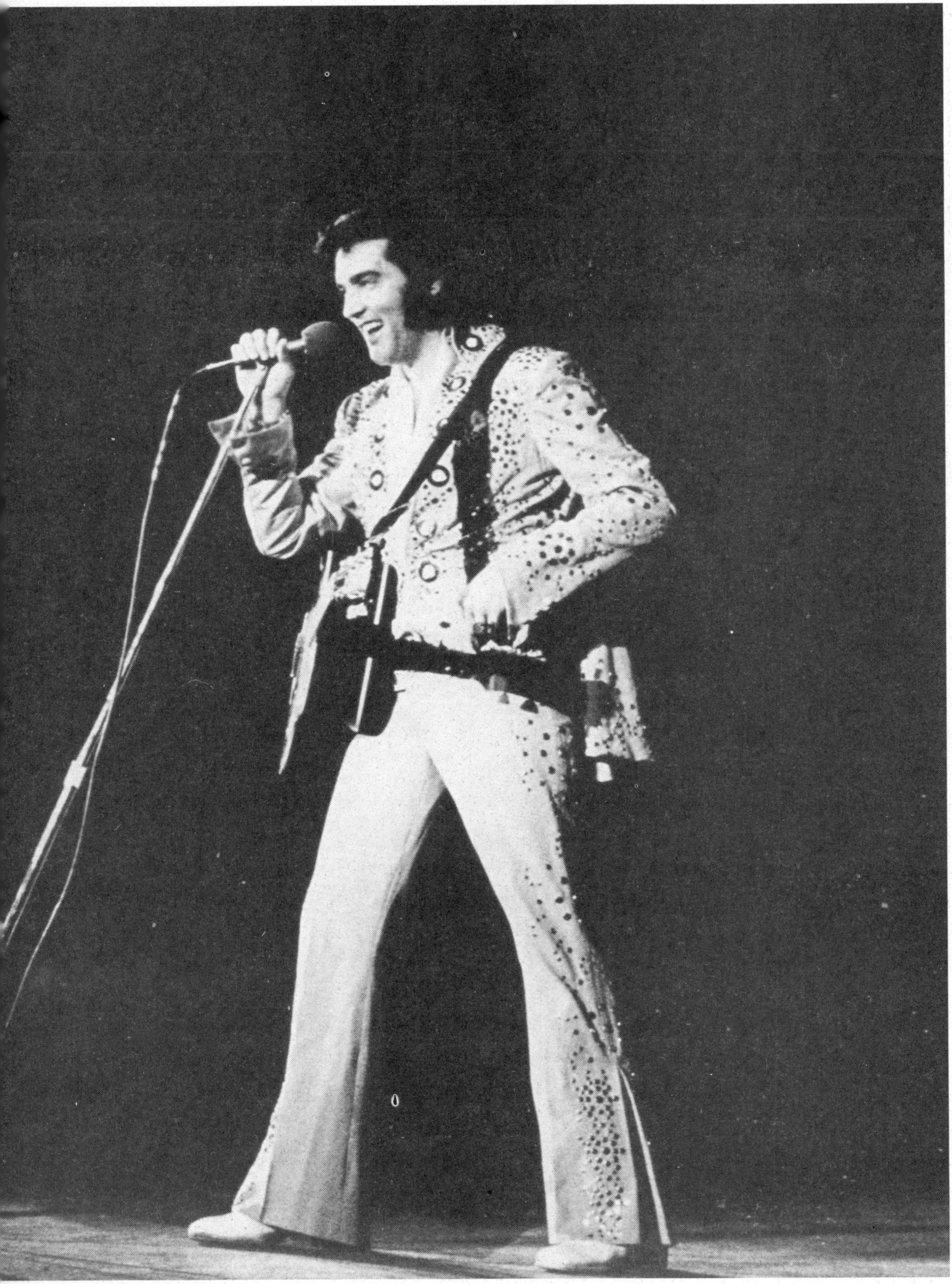

For *THE KING*

This edition exclusively for:
Take That Books
PO Box 200
Harrogate
N. Yorks
HG2 9RB
Tel/Fax: (0423) 507545

Copyright © 1992 Nic van Oudtshoorn
& Maximedia Pty Ltd (A.C.N. 002 666 579)
PO Box 268, Springwood, NSW 2777, Australia.
Tel: (047) 514967, Fax: (047) 515545

ISBN: 0-9519489-0-3

All rights reserved around the world. This publication is copyright and may not be reproduced in any form, in whole or in part in any manner whatever (except excerpts thereof for bona fide purposes in accordance with the Copyright Act) without the prior consent in writing from the Publisher.

While every effort has been made to ensure that the book is free from error or omissions, the Publisher, author and their respective employees or agents shall not accept responsibility for injury, loss of damage occasioned by any person acting or refraining from action as a result of material in this book, whether or not such injury, loss or damage is in any way due to any negligent act or omission, breach of duty or default on the part of the Publisher, author, or their respective employees or agents.

Designed by Mark "Aaron" Elder

Printed and bound by The Book Printer, Maryborough, Victoria, Australia.

CONTENTS

Long Live The King! 8
Viva Lost Elvis! 10
The Ultimate Elvis 16
Clambake! 20
Follow That Car 24
Licence To Thrill 26
Girls! Girls! Girls! 28
The Great Caruso? 30
Hollywood Hound 32
Double Trouble! 38
Is This Elvis? 41
Many Faces of Elvis 48
The Elvis Spotter's Quiz 53
Elvis Identifier! 58
The Elvis Ready Reckoner ... 61
Amazing Elvis! 64
Priscilla Presley Mask! 77
Love Me Tender 89
King Hits 86
Quiz Answers 96
Reward - Terms and Conditions 96

HERE I AM!!

LLV363/9W248 83 22/BULLETIN/LEAD PRESLEY (W245) MEMPHIS, TENNESSEE (AP) - ELVIS PRESLEY, THE MISSISSIPPI-BOY WHOSE COUNTRY ROCK GAITER AND GYRATING HIPS LAUNCHED A NEW STYLE IN POPULAR MUSIC, DIED TUESDAY AFTER AT BAPTIST MEMORIAL HOSPITAL, POLICE SAID, HE WAS 42//MORE//2121G

LONG LIVE THE KING!

★ On 16 August 1977, a Memphis newspaper splashed across its front page the poignant headline: *A lonely life ends on Elvis Presley Boulevard*. Around the world, millions of anguished fans went into mourning for the greatest Rock-'n-Roll star of all time, reported dead at the age of 42 years, seven months, and eight days.

A body said to be that of Elvis Aaron Presley lay in state in Graceland on 17 August 1977, with 80,000 mourners passing by to bid a last farewell to their idol. The next day the coffin was buried at Forest Hill Cemetery in Memphis. Within two weeks three men were arrested at midnight attempting to break into his mausoleum, apparently hunting for the body so they could demand a $10 million ransom. Not long afterwards, for security reasons (or so it was claimed), Elvis' "remains" were transferred to Meditation Gardens at his former home, Graceland.

It was the end of an era - or so it seemed. But within hours of Elvis' "death" being announced, questions were already being asked. Was the body in the coffin really that of the King - or that of a double, or perhaps even a wax dummy? Why was the coffin so unusually heavy? Why did the official report of the County Medical Examiner in Memphis list Elvis' weight as 170 pounds (confirming later that the corpse had, indeed, been weighed during the autopsy), when close friends who saw the King in the "final hours" insist he weighted at least 200 or, more likely, 250 pounds?

There is no doubt that by August 1977 Elvis was tired of being a prisoner to his fame - and that he had long planned to quit around the age of 40. In fact, Elvis himself provided this major clue way back in 1956, when he was starting to climb the ladder of fame. Asked by an interviewer: "And how long can you go on at this hectic pace?", the King replied: "I'm not just sure what you mean by hectic, but I sort of got it blocked out at 40 years. Let's say 39. I won't be able to sing that long but I might be able to act if I ever get to act."

One close associate at Graceland, Daisy M. Williams, who worked for Elvis for nine years, is convinced the King is still alive. "I just find it hard to believe that he died," she confessed to reporters. "There are just too many things that don't seem right. I wish they would dig up that casket and find out what's in it. He used to tell me that he was fed up with everything. 'Daisy,' he said. 'I wish I could take off and live by myself and not tell anybody where I am. Maybe on an island somewhere far away.'"

The King loved life and yet, not long before that fateful August day in 1977, according to stepbrother Billy Stanley, "He called death *the best thing that could happen to you*". Was Elvis talking about real death – or a faked death which would allow him the freedom to assume another identity?

Elvis, by the time he "died", knew a lot more than the average person about death and the way corpses appear, or can be made to appear, in a coffin. He had always been fascinated by the subject of death and, after he split with Linda Thompson, started going to mortuaries regularly and *even practised embalming*. Did he also learn how to substitute and disguise a corpse or a wax dummy to look like him?

In the past 15 years, much has been written and shown on television that suggests there is a more than even chance that ELVIS IS ALIVE! The King has been seen - even photographed - far too many times for anyone to dismiss out of hand the possibility that he may well be alive and well ... and perhaps living next door to you! Even a leading London firm of bookmakers recently dropped the odds against Elvis being found alive, from 5000/1 to 1000/1.

Testimony that Elvis is still alive comes from many sources - Gordon Stoker, leader of Presley's former backing group The Jordanaires, even says he has a letter to prove it. Stoker received the typewritten letter backstage after a concert in Tucson, Arizona, only recently. He's convinced it's from Elvis because the spelling mistakes are the same as those the King always made. Stoker told reporters: **"I now think that the person who was buried was not Elvis. I'm convinced the letter is genuine. He said he loved us all dearly and that he was always thinking of us."**

Finding Elvis could be worth a King's ransom to anyone lucky - or shrewd - enough to track down the star still worshipped by millions of fans around the world as the greatest entertainer in history. In fact, having bought **THE ELVIS SPOTTER'S GUIDE**, you are already in the running for the huge REWARD posted on Page 2.

If you believe the King may be alive, then **THE ELVIS SPOTTER'S GUIDE** is there to help you find him - and have a heap of fun in the process. Compiling the book has taken years of research on five continents to bring you, in words and often exclusive pictures, everything you need to know to track down the King of Rock: his loves and hates, his dreams and fears, his most secret desires ...

There's even a series of six full-colour artist's impressions of the King, based on occupations he personally revealed he would love to follow if ever he could escape the golden cage of stardom.

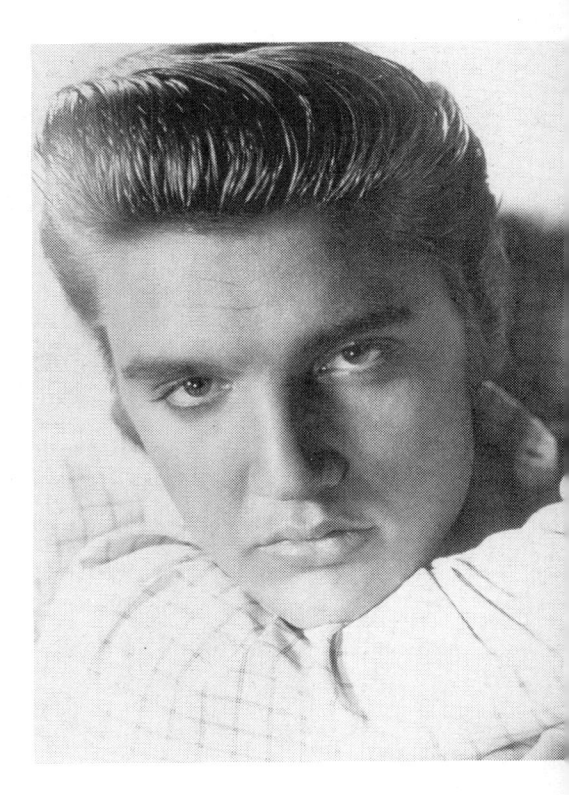

Viva Lost Elvis!

WHERE on earth is Elvis Presley? Ask Michigan grandma Louise Welling and she'll tell you with total conviction: "Right here — in Kalamazoo!"

Louise, who dropped in to the local supermarket with her grandson after church on a sleepy Sunday morning, looked up from the check-out counter and **GOT ALL SHOOK UP** — because there, in the next check-out queue, stood the King of Rock 'n Roll!

"I couldn't believe it!" she gasped to reporters. "I was speechless! I mean, you're not expected to run into Elvis Presley in the grocery store! I was shocked!"

So what did he look like? Elvis, enthused Louise, was thinner, but he still had the same unique looks: from that famous sneer to his jet-black hair and sideburns — he even wore his traditional white jump suit! And that some 11 years after his so-called death...

But that was not the last time this fortunate grandmother saw Elvis. Only a few weeks later, there he was again in Kalamazoo, cruising around in a red Ferrari, after ordering a hamburger "with the lot" at a local Burger King take-away.

Incredible as those early close encounters in a small town may sound, since then more and more evidence that **ELVIS IS ALIVE** has been unearthed by enterprising researchers, tabloid newspapers and TV programs. The King has been spotted, even photographed, in hundreds of places, from the U.S.A. to Australia, Britain, South America ... and most points in between.

ELVIS
Priest discovers secret hideaway

There's no doubt it's HIM!
—Father Hans Von Secker

ELVIS VISTO CUIDANDO LEPROSOS

El 'Rey' enclaustrado dedica su vida por los sufridos

NATIONAL 79¢

ing revelation: ALIVE!

He's performing miracles in a leper colony

HOW A MAJOR Bolivian newspaper first broke the news that The King was alive.

d and his hair was pure white no doubt about it. He was

ement is taken from a letter written an priest to his brother in Berne,

a roar of excitement through the it was made public a few weeks ago.

After telling his brother of conditions in a leper colony located south of the town of El Carmen in Bolivia, and then writing at some length about his own gallbladder problem, Father Hans Von Secker continues:

"My dear Karl, when I first came to this place, I was told there was a white man working with the lepers to the north of here, near the abandoned tin mines at Santa Ana.

Journey

"I resolved therefore, to make the journey to meet this man, whom the natives were calling a saint, and set out in the spring of 1988.

"My long trip took its toll and I felt I was at death's door when I finally reached the leper colony and met the man who cared for them.

"Karl, as God is my witness the man who walked among these lepers, who bandaged their sores and washed their bodies with his own hands, that man was the American, Elvis Presley.

"There is no doubt in my mind.

The old priest described the appalling conditions in the colony, and said that the man he believed to be Elvis was working hard to make things better.

Then he added: "You will remember that we saw Presley in Germany all those years ago when he was serving with the NATO forces.

"Remember how little Bibi swooned and made us get his autograph? (This reference is obscure and may refer to a girlfriend of one of the brothers, or possibly a family member — Editor).

"But you would have trouble recognizing him.

"The King is a living saint," declares the holy father

His hair was pure white, thinning at the front, and at some time recently he had broken his right leg.

"It had healed badly, making it some inches shorter than the other, so he walked with a limp and it was obvious that every step pained him.

"Yet he was unflagging in his devotion to our stricken brethren. He worked with the lepers, ate with them, slept with them and when the time came he buried them.

"When I talked with him I realized with a shock that though his work had aged him terribly, his eyes were still bright and young, shining with life and good humor."

Father Von Secker then spoke to Elvis, but the conversation was brief. He wrote:

God's Divine Will

"Presley told me that for the first time in his life he was doing something worthwhile. And he added: 'I came to this place because it was God's Divine Will.'

"To my utter disappointment he would tell me no more.

"In fact, when I woke up the morning after my arrival he was gone.

"I asked the lepers where the white man was and they replied that he had traveled north where there were other lepers to be cared for. They also said that he had a mission to preach the word of Christ.

"On the night of my arrival, as we talked, Elvis touched me lightly on the chest and said: 'You have trouble. There.'

"Karl, from that day to this my gallbladder has given me no further trouble. Elvis performed a true

"...as God is my witness, that man was the American, Elvis Presley..."

> Gott sei mein Zeuge, der Mann den ich unter den armen Aussätzigen gesehen habe, der die eckeligen Wunden verband und ihre kranken Körper mit seinen eigenen Händen wusch, der Mann war der Amerikaner Elvis Presley

Location of leper colony

SOUTH AMERICA
BOLIVIA
Santa Ana
SOUTH ATLANTIC OCEAN

MAP SHOWS the location of the leper colony.

miracle that day.

"I believe Elvis Presley is still in Bolivia, still tending the lepers, still performing miracles and still preaching the gospel.

"Is he a saint? That I don't know. Certainly that man was filled with an inner glow that could only come from the grace of God.

"I truly believe he was walking in the shoes of the fisherman!"

Missionary work

According to Karl Von Secker, his brother, the priest, left Bolivia in July of last year and is now doing missionary work in the Gran Chaco wilderness of Paraguay.

Church officials say they plan to investigate Father Von Secker's revelation "in the near future."

In many of these accounts, Elvis does look different ... but there's little doubt that's probably part of his disguise, because the eye-witnesses all agree it's **HIM**. And the reason they're so confident is simple: there's no mistaking that old "Pelvis" sex appeal that so often created mass hysteria, particularly among women.

As part of the quest for the **HIDDEN ELVIS**, it is essential to look closely at the places and faces of these sightings, because they could provide vital clues on where to find Elvis today — and then tempt him into revealing himself.

☞ *In Texas, he appeared with blond hair and wearing contact lenses that made his eyes a brilliant blue.*

☞ *In Hawaii, the King (always keen on law-enforcement) was seen with a dome that could have been borrowed from Kojak. He was back to his top weight and was wearing a colourful woman's robe known to locals as a muu-muu.*

☞ *He has even been seen back at Graceland - where in the witching hours before dawn a dedicated couple of fans saw a mysterious stretch limo pull up and a figure that could only be the King get out and disappear through those famous Music Gates.*

No-one believed a pretty Atlanta barmaid when she told how she romanced Elvis for three years **AFTER** his so-called death — yet when she took a lie-detector test, she passed with ease. Elizabeth Prince met a man touring Holiday Inns doing Willy Nelson covers and fell in love ... only to discover that the new bearded face and sandy hair actually belonged to the King, the result of years of painstaking plastic surgery! Their love affair ended when **THE MAN** vanished into the "wild west" as mysteriously as he had arrived. Laments Elizabeth: "Elvis' death is the greatest cover-up since Watergate!"

In Scotland, Elvis was seen by amazed drinkers

"I'm just so tired of being Elvis Presley."

- Elvis to Felton Jarvis (his RCA producer).

ERY ONE CALL

vidence King is alive!

ELVIS IS STILL ALIVE

POLICE COMPUTER scientists have verified that a photograph taken seven years after Elvis Presley's supposed death is almost certainly that of the singing idol.

The 1984 newspaper picture — showing Elvis, Muhammed Ali, and Jesse Jackson — was taken to British experts to authenticate after a leading investigator was unable to locate scientists in this country willing to undertake the task.

"We tried our best to prove it wasn't Mr Presley, but we couldn't do it," confessed one of the experts with the top secret computer company which specializes in image analysis and uses the most advanced techniques in the world.

The company and the scientists are considered so important to national security that it is against British law to print their names. The company does top-secret work for the British Defence Ministry and Scotland Yard.

The experts, who usually work on enhancing blurred and long distance images to identify spies and criminals, were intrigued by the prospect of examining the picture, taken seven years after Elvis' reported death in 1977.

State-of-the-art

Through high-level contacts in the ministry, the EXAMINER was able to obtain authorization for the company to proceed with the state-of-the-art analysis of the picture, which has only recently surfaced.

The photo was taken by a United Press International photographer. It shows Muhammed Ali leaving Columbia Presbyterian Hospital in New York City after being treated for Parkinson's disease. Also shown with Ali are presidential candidate Jesse Jackson, an unidentified black man, and a man with a stunning resemblance to Elvis.

POLICE COMPUTER SCIENTIST experts tried their best to prove the man in the photo WASN'T Elvis Presley, but couldn't do it.

— claim police experts

enough to work with to draw a startling conclusion.

"We used every computer device to prove the photo was a fake, or that the man simply bore a resemblance to Mr Presley," said a senior spokesman for the company.

"But there's no way we can be certain it isn't him. The likeness to Mr Presley is incredible. It certainly could be Mr Presley. In fact, the odds are overwhelming that it is Mr Presley."

Features

Another scientist who worked on the photo analysis said: "We have developed our own sophisticated methods of enhancing photographs, using computers to either make features stand out or fade into a background.

"Taking an image on the screen from a photo, we can change shades, play around with angles, measure noses, chins, and parts of the face to minute fractions.

"We compared this photo with dozens of known images of Mr Presley and the similarities in the face are stunning."

The picture ran in the Cincinnati Post sports section on September 21, 1984. It was distributed on the UPI photo wire. At the time, the similarity to Elvis

went unnoticed as attention was focused on Ali and his battle with Parkinson's disease.

But the growing underground of Elvis fans who believe he is alive began to circulate the picture a few months ago.

Investigation

Leading the investigation into the picture have been Gail Giorgio, author of the best-seller Is Elvis Alive? (Tudor Publishing) and Major Bill Smith, author of Memphis Mystery (LeCam Publications). Both believe that Elvis faked his death in 1977 with help from the federal government to escape a death contract from the Mafia.

Giorgio urged the EXAMINER to seek analysis of the photo outside the US, because convinced that federal

THE PHOTOGRAPH taken seven years after Elvis Presley's alleged death.

has silenced experts here.

Giorgio pointed out the strong bond between Ali and Elvis.

"Elvis visited Ali's training camp several times before championship fights," Giorgio said. "At Graceland, there is a set of boxing gloves on display that Ali gave Elvis.

Spiritual bond

"Elvis gave Ali a beautiful robe. They shared a deep spiritual bond and had tremendous respect for each other."

Even more intriguing is the fact that Ali owns a large horse farm in Berrian Springs, Michigan — just out...

certain the picture is genuine.

He showed the photo at a recent Elvis contest in Dallas, Texas where fans unanimously said the man in it was The King.

Another Elvis investigator, Steve Albert, a disc jockey at a Brockton, Massachusetts, radio station, told the EXAMINER his research has revealed that Elvis was deeply involved with Drug Enforcement Administration.

"He had an undercover agent traveling with him..."

Elvis

law enforcement, ...rigue, and I think ...to have done some...ike that."

...s Nicholson: "If it ...e that Elvis Presley ...live, my book would ...tty close to the truth ...w it was done."

...adds: "In my busi... there's nothing im... at all about someone ...ng.

...ust because it could ...Elvis doesn't mean any... to me."

...icholson says several ...dred copies of his novel ...vanished just weeks af... they appeared in two ...lifornia bookstores.

The bookstores, he con...nds, could not account ...r the missing books. Just few were sold.

Fiction

"I'm starting to get the impression that people are trying to keep my book out of the hands of the public, even though it's only fiction," says Nicholson, who claims to have received phone calls telling him to drop any further promotion of his book.

He adds: "Maybe some Elvis memorabilia people are afraid they're going to be cut out of a large piece of the pie if this thing takes hold."

When asked if Elvis could be suppressing the novel, Nicholson replied: "The guy was such a phenomenon and had so many contacts, I think he could do anything he wanted."

—EDWARD...

S WANTED

ELVIS IS ALIVE
ADMIT POLICE EXPERTS

...after analyzing this incredible photograph

75¢ NEW OR

NATIONAL

(who later all swore to having consumed only "a wee dram ... or three") as he dashed into the Gents at a Glasgow pub. Not long after, in England, he was reported on the motorway near Bristol test-driving a Skoda car — an amazing come-down from his prized Stutz but perfect as a disguise.

☞ **One of the most recent reported sightings was in Augusta, Georgia, where housewife Margaret Moore actually spoke to the King as he was about to get into a white Cadillac. He told her he had written over 200 songs since "going into hiding" - and that he would soon release one called "Take the Time to Love Yourself". Elvis expert William Stern, who has checked out more than 200 Elvis sightings since 1977, said all evidence pointed out to this being a GENUINE ENCOUNTER.**

Elvis has not only been seen - he's also been heard quite often, making telephone calls and sending tape recordings to fans. One of the most authoritative accounts comes from former US Air Force Major Bill Smith, of Fort Worth, Texas. After "regular" contact by phone with the King for years, Major Smith has written a book telling how Elvis faked his own death. He explained to a reporter from the *Houston Chronicle*: "Elvis wants me to tell the world the truth. I'm the closest man in the world to him... I talked to him on the phone about six weeks ago and he said big things are gonna happen soon and I was gonna be part of it. I feel like he's coming back."

In his book, *Elvis After Life*, Dr Raymond Moody of Atlanta tells the amazing story of how Elvis had actually appeared in a hospital ward and helped a woman get through labour.

In the pages that follow are some of the stories that told the world **ELVIS LIVES!** A careful reading could provide that elusive clue that could lead you to the HIDEOUT of the King...

His secret hideout revealed

By ROBERT BOYD

...walks.

...feat was became apparent when an ...ed to question the few rural neighbors ...let loose two large, ferocious dogs on ...ed to race back to his car before their

...tions by pointing a shotgun at the re-...operty and out of the county.

...aywhere close to the secluded property ...was seen minutes later speeding off in ...m where Elvis is in hiding.

...arm by another Elvis researcher who ... Rumors of Elvis' location had reached ...rm the approximate location. It was ob-...ed, and almost inaccessible. It was ob-...ime farmland is not being worked and ... spread is horse breeding — always one

...he alias Johnny Buford?

...oned dozens of people in surrounding ...resting fact to emerge was that Elvis was ...ng the alias Johnny Buford.

...Dogwood Inn in Oneonta, Alabama, posi-...they were shown as Johnny Buford. ..., sure," said cashier Glenda Scott. "He ...ot, but we haven't seen him in several ...he looked a lot like Elvis. He must be over

...the inn volunteered that Johnny Buford ...mself, although he was always polite and

...-selling books on The King, Is Elvis Alive? ...uford fits into the pattern Elvis has used. ...nitials. His secret name which people used ...as Johnny Burrows. In fact, that was his ...(Drug Enforcement Agency). He also went ...ron."

...was the name Elvis had selected for his child ...a boy, according to noted Elvis expert Clif-...o said that Elvis was a strong believer in law ...and order and considered himself a pa-...triot who was fighting illegal drugs by providing information to federal authorities.

When the Mafia found out what he had been doing, he was as good as dead.

Said Giorgio: "Elvis was brave and possibly would not have yielded to threats, but shortly before his faked death he received a note warning that Lisa Marie's head was going to be served to him on a platter. I think that's when he decided he had to act to save his precious nine-year-old daughter.

"That area in Alabama makes sense for a place for him to start a new life. He is basically a country boy and he loves horses. He had a horse ranch

ELVIS FAKED his death to escape death threats from drug-dealing thugs.

He certainly has the money to pay them, and they probably would have wanted to help once they found out the danger he was in.

"Don't forget he had the full help of the federal government in providing cover and a new identity. He is probably better protected than anyone in the Federal

vis' hometown of Tupelo, Mississippi, and less than 170 miles from his Graceland mansion in Memphis, Tennessee.

Dozens of people interviewed in surrounding towns said they remember seeing a person who resembled Elvis Presley.

"Sure, I've seen a guy who looks like him," Jim Yager, owner of the

to himself, but he's been in here."

Edwina Bryan, the postmistress of Cleveland, said it would be easy for someone like Elvis to conceal his identity.

"We require no proof to set up a mail route," Edwina said. "Also, he could have people pick

---

"And how long can you go on at this hectic pace?", an interviewer asked Elvis in 1956. He replied: "I'm not just sure what you mean by hectic, but I sort of got it blocked out at 40 years. Let's say 39. I won't be able to sing that long but I might be able to act if I ever get to act."

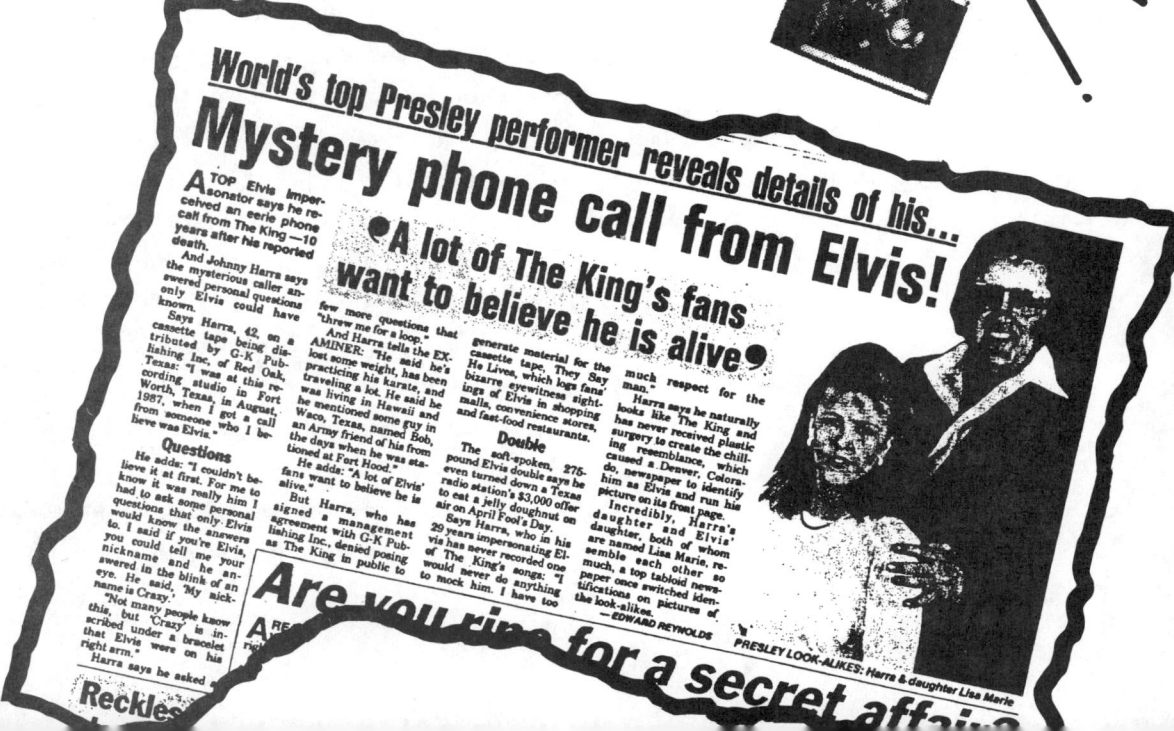

WORLD EXCLUSIVE

Top investigators track down The King

MORE PHOTOS INSIDE

World's top Presley performer reveals details of his...

Mystery phone call from Elvis!

● A lot of The King's fans want to believe he is alive●

A TOP Elvis impersonator says he received an eerie phone call from The King — 10 years after his reported death.

And Johnny Harra says the mysterious caller answered personal questions only Elvis could have known.

Says Harra, 42, on a cassette tape being distributed by G-K Publishing Inc. of Red Oak, Texas: "I was at this recording studio in Fort Worth, Texas, in August 1987, when I got a call from someone who I believe was Elvis."

Questions

He adds: "I couldn't believe it at first. For me to know it was really him I had to ask some personal questions that only Elvis would know the answers to. I said if you're Elvis you could tell me your nickname and he answered in the blink of an eye. He said, 'My nickname is Crazy.'

"Not many people know this, but 'Crazy' is inscribed under a bracelet that Elvis wore on his right arm."

Harra says he asked a few more questions that "threw me for a loop."

And Harra tells the EXAMINER: He said he's lost some weight, has been practicing his karate, and traveling a lot. He said he was living in Hawaii and he mentioned some guy in Waco, Texas, named Bob, an Army friend of his from the days when he was stationed at Fort Hood."

He adds: "A lot of Elvis' fans want to believe he is alive."

But Harra, who has signed a management agreement with G-K Publishing Inc., denied posing as The King in public to generate material for the cassette tape. They Say He Lives, which logs fans' bizarre eyewitness sightings of Elvis in shopping malls, convenience stores, and fast-food restaurants.

Double

The soft-spoken, 275-pound Elvis double says he even turned down a Texas radio station's $3,000 offer to eat a jelly doughnut on air on April Fool's Day.

Says Harra, who in his 29 years impersonating Elvis has never recorded one of The King's songs: "I would never do anything to mock him. I have too much respect for the man.

Harra says he naturally looks like The King and has never received plastic surgery to create the chilling resemblance, which caused a Denver, Colorado, newspaper to identify him as Elvis and run his picture on its front page.

Incredibly, Harra's daughter and Elvis' daughter, both of whom are named Lisa Marie, resemble each other so much, a top tabloid newspaper once switched identifications on pictures of the look-alikes.

— EDWARD REYNOLDS

PRESLEY LOOK-ALIKES: Harra & daughter Lisa Marie

THE ULTIMATE ELVIS

★ Sniffing out THE INTIMATE ELVIS is not a job for a HOUND DOG - it calls for great detective work and an intimate knowledge of the King of Rock.

So here is all you need to know about his favourites, from FOOD and CARS to his GUNS, his GIRLS (lots of them), his MUSIC and his MOVIES. It's the kind of information that could give Elvis away - no matter how perfect his disguise.

During your quest, always keep in mind what the King would do in certain circumstances - like getting acquainted with a girl. For example, if that stranger you suspect is Elvis acts in the following way, chances are you've snared the King:

"Just get her attention," Elvis once explained to his close friends. "Then, if the girl shows any interest in you for whatever reason ... explore it! Don't shy away. And don't worry what you'll say to them. Just say, 'How do you feel about it?' When they state their position, just hold their hand and say, 'That's just about what I was feeling.' It works every time! And boys, there's a bonus. Sometimes they'll tell you things you never even thought of."

Or take eating. Elvis has certain ingrained habits he may well slip back into despite the most elaborate disguise. So look out for a familiar looking stranger who, even at table, always eats solid food like sausages, bacon, chops, even steak, with his bare fingers - while daintily holding his little finger erect in the air!

When it comes to guns, the King has one major weakness - he likes to shoot up TV sets! When Elvis gets bored with a TV program, or angry because the set is not producing a perfect picture, he likes to grab a gun (and there are always plenty around the King) and take a pot shot or six at the offending set! When Elvis was on tour, smashed TV sets were regularly added to the hotel bill.

If you hear of someone who likes to hire an entire movie theatre for himself and his friends at midnight, it's an odds-on bet you've found Elvis. Try to get to one of those showings: if that familiar stranger is there and *insists that his girfriend sits on his left*, you can bet you've cornered the King!

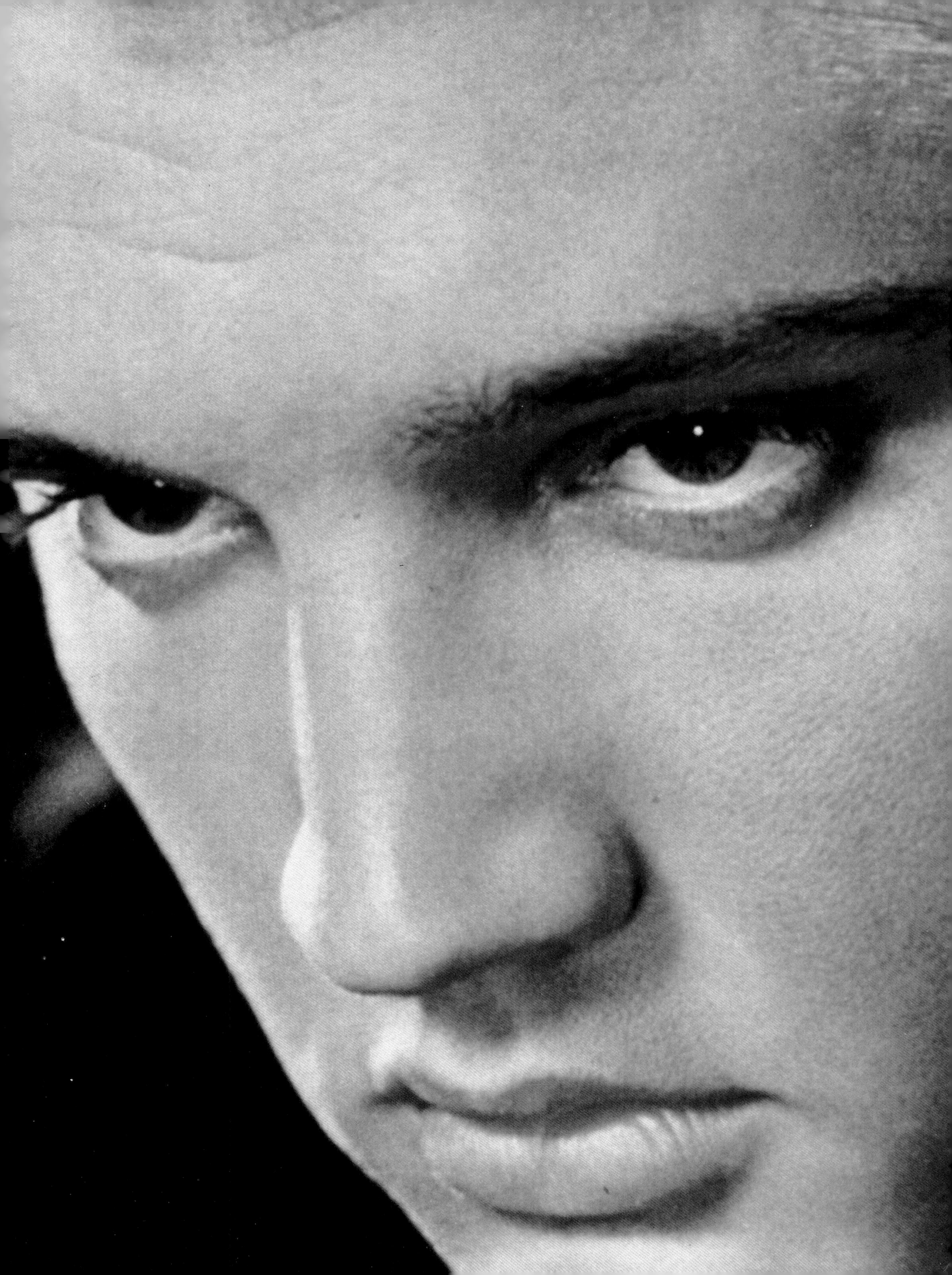

ELVIS Today?

"Pastor Aaron healed me, hallelujah! I was overweight and addicted to junk food and tranquil-lsers. But he said, 'Man, I know what you're going through. You need to escape from the past, but remember, always love your mama.' Then I went to a far-away country and spoke up for the Lord. Hallelujah!!"

— Jessie G. Vernon, 59.

* "I should have been a preacher. I should have stayed with the church" - Elvis to Nancy Sinatra after the birth of Lisa Marie.

ELVIS Today?

"When the King first came to me, man he was a wreck! After intensive training in our mountain retreat, he became a lean and mean machine."
— Me Kan Wok, Great Green Dragon of the mysterious Hai Iki Thump Order

* Elvis, whose karate name is Tiger, holds an eighth-degree black belt.

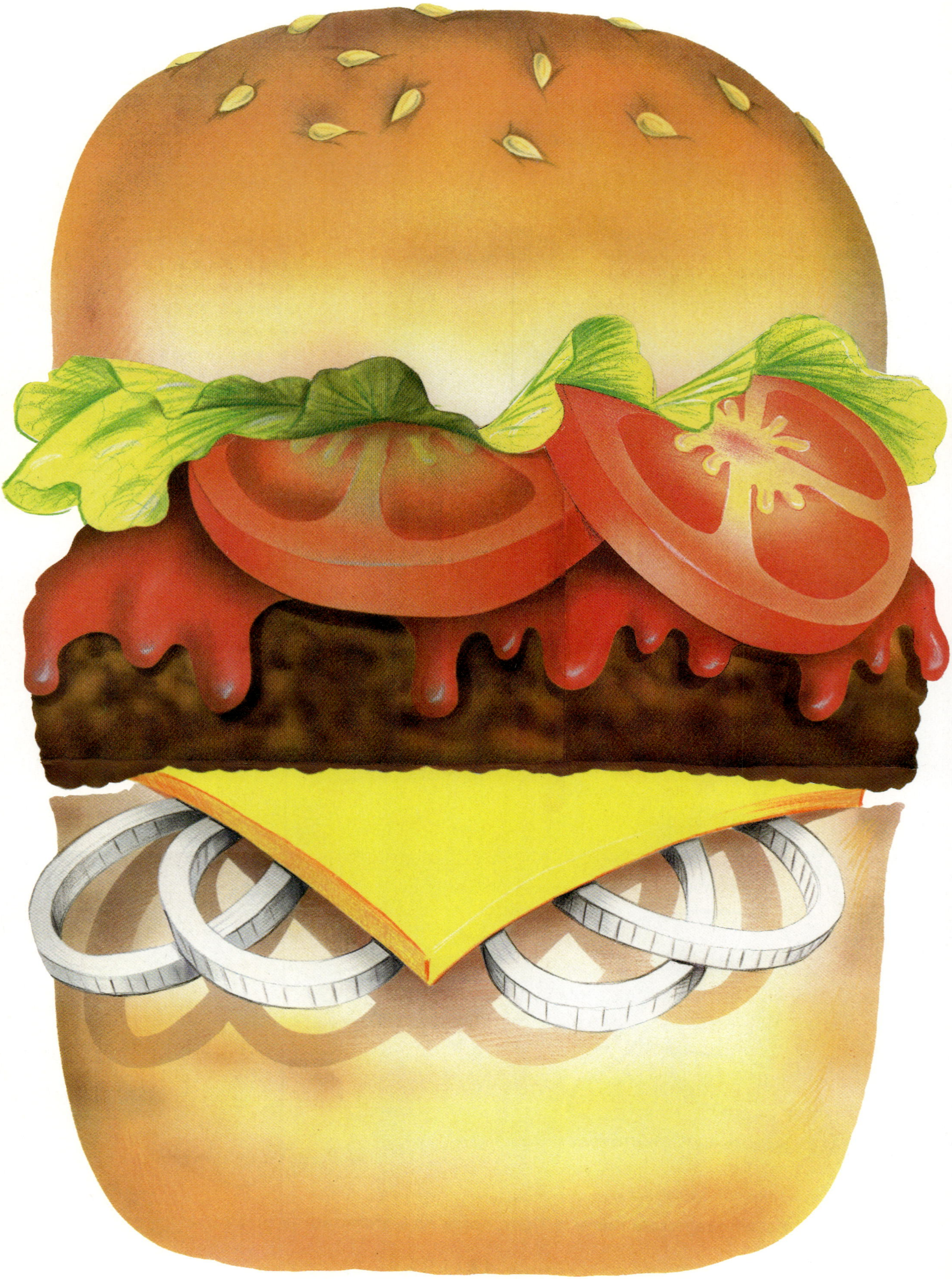

Clambake!

⭐ Elvis loves to eat — but his taste has always been eccentric, to say the least. So tempting him out of hiding with a TENDER steak won't work — you'll need the taste treats below to cook up a feast fit for the attention of the King.

IMPORTANT: Remember to make the portions truly King-size, too!

Snacks

Five or six **PEANUT-BUTTER-AND-BANANA SANDWICHES** fried in butter or toasted under the grill.

FRIED BACON-AND-POTATO SANDWICHES: Fry bacon strips until they start to burn. Fry thick slices of potatoes and onion rings in the bacon fat until brown. Place on thick slices of bread, spread thickly with mustard and make sandwiches which are browned under the griller.

Breakfast

A **SPANISH OMELET** made with at least six eggs, twenty strips of bacon burnt to a crisp, a big bowl of hash-brown potatoes and a giant jug of freshly squeezed orange juice.

COFFEE must be served boiling hot and extra strong. And remember: No talking at all before the second cup.

Lunch

Six or more **CHEESEBURGERS** made with thick strips of very crisp bacon instead of hamburger meat.

GOOD OL' SOUTHERN CORN PONE: The movie *Clambake* did not make Elvis crave seafood, but triggered off a deep-seated desire for a typical Southern dish - corn pone. For almost a month his cook from the Deep South had to make pan after pan of the rich, heavy food, which Elvis would dunk into a brimming bowl of buttermilk before eating it in huge quantities.

Dinner

MEATLOAF 'N MASH: "There was a period when [Elvis] ate meatloaf, mashed potatoes, gravy and sliced tomatoes for dinner every single

Clue No. 57

Yes or no?

Would Elvis eat this?

night," recalls Marty Lecker, one of the Memphis Mafia. "He kept up this routine for two years!"

COTTON' PICKIN TUMMY TREAT: Mix together into a gooey mess the following: mashed potatoes covered in "thickenin' gravy", crisply fried King Cotton bacon, sauerkraut, chowder peas, sliced tomatoes. Tuck in with a spoon for the soft stuff and your bare hands for the bacon — and the King, if he's nearby, will come running, salivating like a true HOUND DOG.

Sweets

Elvis' favourite **ICE-CREAMS** are Eskimo Pies, Fudgesicles, Dreamsickles and Nutty Buddys.

Recently, an American newspaper unearthed a major scoop: Elvis' favourite pound cake recipe! It's called the **ELVIS PRESLEY WHIPPING CREAM POUND CAKE** and requires:

3 cups sugar
half pound softened butter
7 eggs, room temperature
3 cups cake flour, sift twice
1 cup whipping cream
2 teaspoons vanilla extract

Butter and flour a 10-inch tube pan. Thoroughly cream together sugar and butter. Add eggs, one at a time, beating well with each addition. Mix in half of the flour, then the whipping cream, then the other half of the flour. Add vanilla. Pour batter into prepared pan, set in cold oven and turn heat to 350 deg.rees F. Bake one hour to seventy minutes until a sharp knife inserted in cake comes out clean. Cool in pan five minutes. Remove from pan and cool. Thoroughly wrapped, this cake will keep several days.

Fruit

Iced **WATERMELON** is a particular Elvis favourite. At Graceland he and the Memphis Mafia regularly cut out the sweet red hearts and competed to see who could eat the most — and also who could create the prettiest pattern on the carpet by spitting out the pips on the ground.

Ripe **HONEYDEW AND YOGHURT** has long been the King's health food diet. So if your Elvis suspect looks like he's on a health kick, try this as a temptation.

Drinks

Elvis does not generally like alcohol, but loves cola, which he used to drink in great quantities while watching movies at midnight after renting an entire movie theatre for himself and close friends.

Foods that will NOT tempt Elvis

"When I saw all that **STUFFED LOBSTER** and big roasts of **BLOODY MEAT**, it made me sick." Elvis' own words, after attending a New York music publisher's dinner in his honour, speak for themselves.

Follow That Car!

★ The King and cars have always been synonymous. "I like cars. All kinds. I have my Cads and my Lincolns and my Messerschmitt and now I have another. A little red racer. Seats one." That came from Elvis back in 1957 – and he has remained a lifelong car fanatic, both as an owner and as a donor. The King loves to give away cars almost as much as he loves buying and driving them, so if you do track him down, chances are you'll end up with at least a Cadillac for your trouble.

For instance, Elvis bought a Caddy (then priced at $13,000) for a Colorado TV reporter because he liked the way Don Kinney had presented a story about Elvis' gift of luxury cars to four policemen. Kinney had ended the story with the comment, "I wouldn't mind an economy car..." Minutes later he received a call from Elvis, who said there was a Cadillac Seville waiting for him at a local dealer!

During that same January 1976 holiday in Vale, Colorado, Elvis gave away a total of five cars – to absolute strangers.

There are certain cars the King just cannot resist, so if you want to attract his attention, rent, borrow or buy one and cruise the streets slowly, all the time checking the reaction of bystanders for that stare that could betray Elvis.

The King has always been a **CADILLAC MAN**. With his first royalty cheque, he bought a hot pink Caddy for his mother, and by 1958 he owned four of these gas guzzlers: one pink-and-black, another canary yellow, one white and one plain black.

☞ *The best bet is a Stutz Blackhawk, preferably a 1971 model, or a 1973 Stutz Blackhawk Custom. Elvis bought his first imported Blackhawk for $100,000 on September 1971, and he owned two by the time he "died". If you can't get (or can't afford) one of those, try a 1967 Ferrari, preferably in black, or any Cadillac, although a 1955 Fleetwood would give you that extra edge on the other Elvis spotters.*

Elvis even featured a song called "Pink Cadillac" in his early shows – and he slipped a reference to a pink Cadillac into the lyrics when he recorded "Baby, Let's Play House".

Elvis' first car was a 1942 Lincoln Zephyr like that above which his father bought him as an 18th birthday gift.

SPOTTING TIP: When the King buys cars, he buys big — so keep in touch with luxury car dealers and check up on anyone whose spending pattern resembles this:

In September 1973, Elvis went on a car shopping spree, walking into Schelling Lincoln in Memphis to buy five Continental Mark IVs for $60,000.

In July 1975, the King lashed out on fourteen Cadillacs — and two aircraft to keep them company.

A sports car - a 1971 De Tomaso Pantera - which Elvis bought for girlfriend Linda Thompson in 1974 for $2500, was sold in 1981 for $2 million. It comes complete with three bullet holes, which Elvis fired into the car after he got mad one morning when it would not start.

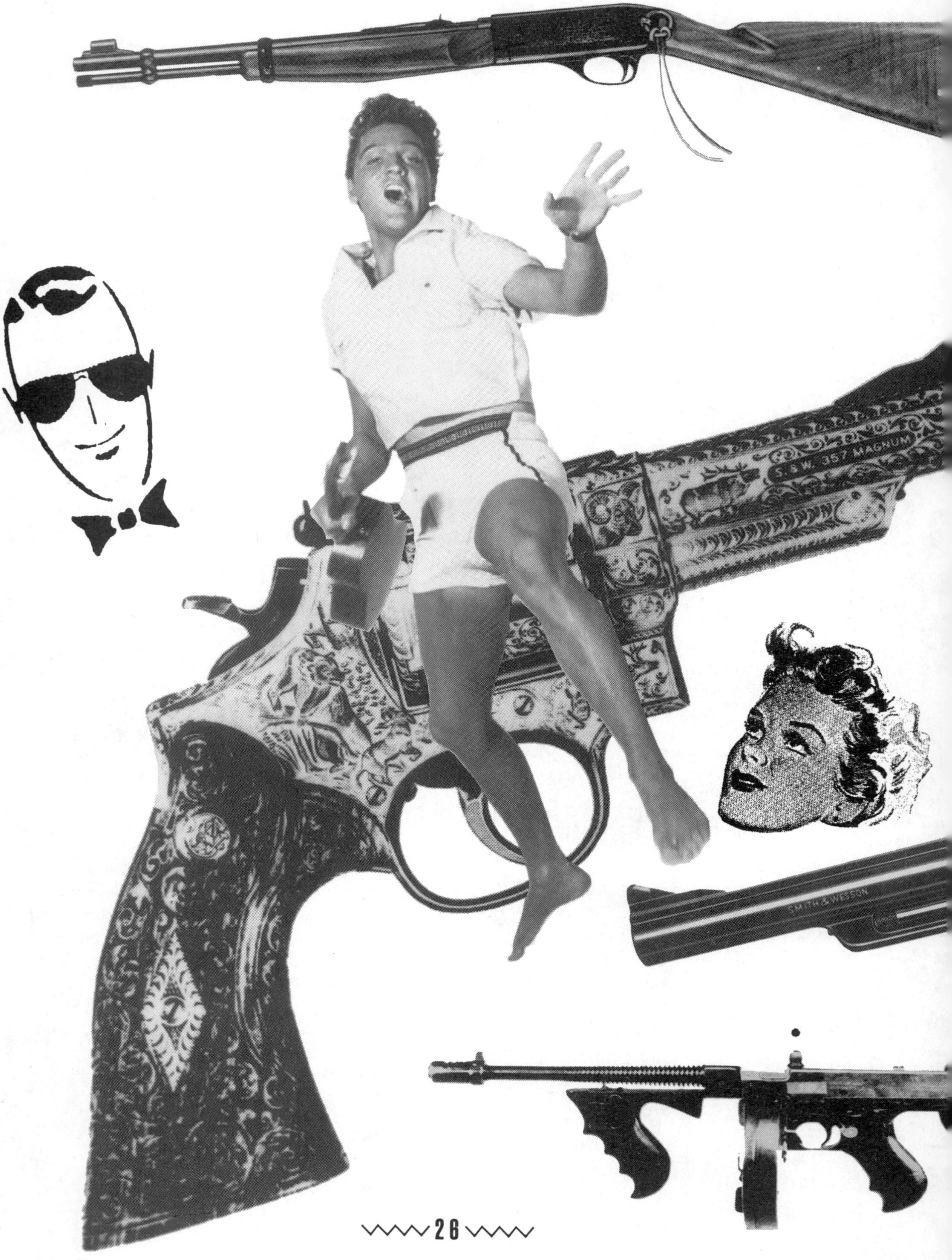
S. & W. 357 MAGNUM
SMITH & WESSON

Licence To Thrill!

★ If you're looking for Elvis, look for guns. The King is never without one, or more usually, two or three, handguns. These range from a four-shot Derringer he always carries in his boot, even on stage, to his favourite, a .38 Magnum, which like Clint Eastwood he likes to wear in a bulging shoulder holster.

When he "died", Elvis owned 37 guns and rifles, including a sawn-off shot-gun. His firearms were everywhere: in his cars, his homes, his bedroom, even beside his plate at mealtimes.

So what kind of guns should you look out for when you meet that stranger who may just be Elvis? Here are some of his favourites:

- ✓ Gold-inlaid .375 Colt Python revolver;
- ✓ Colt .45, preferably the company's 50th anniversary model stamped with the dates 1917-1967;
- ✓ Gold-plated .44 Ruger Blackhawk;
- ✓ .22 calibre machine gun with a horizontal drum, preferably the classic designed by Dick Casule of Salt Lake City;
- ✓ 1927-model .45 calibre Tommy Gun, with a perpendicular drum and slotted muzzle brake (according to one report, Elvis obtained his from "his friends in the Chicago Mob");
- ✓ .300 calibre Magnum assassination rifle, complete with telescopic sight, which can be broken down to fit inside an attache case;
- ✓ Pearl-handled Patton .45;
- ✓ Mauser Luger machine pistol from WWII;
- ✓ Walther PPK/S double-action automatic;
- ✓ 19th century Carl Hauptmann-Ferlach double-barrelled hunting rifle (Elvis' was once owned by Hermann Goering, and featured a barrel chased in gold, and a walnut stock, hand-carved and inlaid with ivory);
- ✓ Pearl-handled 9mm "James Bond" Beretta.

Elvis did not stay in HEARTBREAK HOTEL for long after being rejected by Debra Paget - soon his favourite fun was racing cars along the highway on his motorcycle with Natalie Wood seated behind him. She recalls: "We'd go to P.C. Brown's and have a hot fudge sundae. We'd go to Hamburger Hamlet and have a burger and a Coke. He didn't drink. He didn't swear. He didn't even smoke! It was like having the date that I never ever had in high school. I thought it was really wild!"

Girls! Girls! Girls! Girls!

⭐ ELVIS made three movies containing the word GIRLS — and he has always loved women as much as they love him! To check out the kind of girls that appeal to the King — so you can plant a look-alike to attract his attention — study the pictures of the girls on these pages and throughout the book. And remember, thanks to *The Elvis Spotter's Guide*, even a male can now impersonate Priscilla by cutting out and wearing, preferably in dim light, our exclusive **PRISCILLA MASK** that appears on pages 78 and 79.

Elvis married only once, but he proposed to at least two other girls: **DEBRA PAGET**, his co-star in *Love Me Tender,* who turned him down because of parental pressure; and **GINGER ALDEN**, who says they became engaged on 26 January 1977, chosen for its numerological significance.

Elvis' favourite female co-star was Nancy Sinatra, in the film Speedway. "She's difficult to get along with, but she's my kinda gal," he said.

"Elvis' reputation will never die!" - Ann Margret, who co-starred with the King in Viva Las Vegas.

"She looks like an angel!" That was Elvis the GI's first reaction on seeing 14-year-old Priscilla Beaulieu in August 1959. They were married in Las Vegas on 1 May 1967 - a replica of their wedding cake is at Graceland - and divorced on 9 October 1973.

The Great Caruso?

★ What kind of **MUSIC** should you play to attract the attention of the King? Rock 'n Roll or The Great Caruso singing Italian Opera?

Surprisingly, some of both — Elvis was an avid collector of the records of the great Italian tenor. He became a fan after seeing Mario Lanza in the movie *The Great Caruso*.

Deep South spiritual music has always been a Presley favourite (he recorded many throughout his career), because to Elvis, that was where his inspiration came from.

"The first thing I could remember in my life was sittin' on my mama's lap in church," he explained. "What did I know when I was two years old? But all I wanted to do was run down the aisle and go sing with the choir. I knew it then; I had to sing. ... Those people in church know how to move. They're free. They're not afraid to move their bodies, and that's where I got it. When I started singing, I just did what came natural, what they taught me. God is natural.

"The coloured folks have been singing it and playing it just the same way I'm doing now man, for more years than I know. Nobody paid it no mind till I goosed it up."

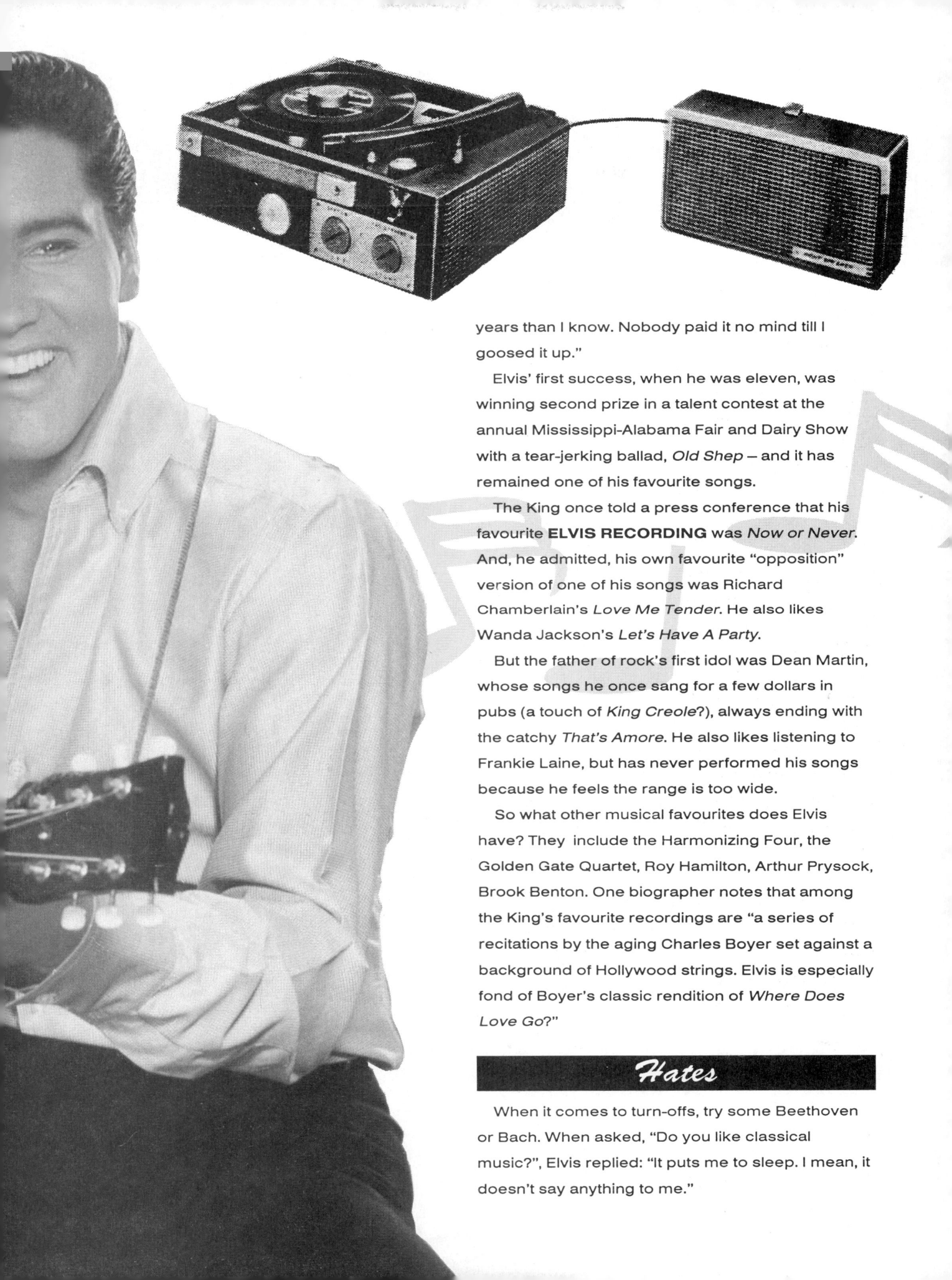

Elvis' first success, when he was eleven, was winning second prize in a talent contest at the annual Mississippi-Alabama Fair and Dairy Show with a tear-jerking ballad, *Old Shep* — and it has remained one of his favourite songs.

The King once told a press conference that his favourite **ELVIS RECORDING** was *Now or Never*. And, he admitted, his own favourite "opposition" version of one of his songs was Richard Chamberlain's *Love Me Tender*. He also likes Wanda Jackson's *Let's Have A Party*.

But the father of rock's first idol was Dean Martin, whose songs he once sang for a few dollars in pubs (a touch of *King Creole*?), always ending with the catchy *That's Amore*. He also likes listening to Frankie Laine, but has never performed his songs because he feels the range is too wide.

So what other musical favourites does Elvis have? They include the Harmonizing Four, the Golden Gate Quartet, Roy Hamilton, Arthur Prysock, Brook Benton. One biographer notes that among the King's favourite recordings are "a series of recitations by the aging Charles Boyer set against a background of Hollywood strings. Elvis is especially fond of Boyer's classic rendition of *Where Does Love Go*?"

Hates

When it comes to turn-offs, try some Beethoven or Bach. When asked, "Do you like classical music?", Elvis replied: "It puts me to sleep. I mean, it doesn't say anything to me."

Hollywood Hound!

⭐ After screen testing Elvis in April 1956 and signing him to a $450,000 deal to make three films over seven years, producer Hal Wallis enthused: "I had the same thrill on seeing Errol Flynn for the first time."

He was right — Elvis was a box-office sensation from his first movie, *Love Me Tender,* released in October 1956, to his last, *Change Of Habit,* and the 29 in between. Unique to Hollywood, no Elvis movie EVER made a loss.

"I've never seen anything like it," Ben, the white-haired major domo of the big silver gates at Paramount Studios in Hollywood, told the magazine *Photoplay* in 1961. "I've been at this gate for thirty years, and I've seen 'em come and go ... Dietrich, Chevalier, Barrymore, Jimmy Dean, all the rest. But I've never, in all my born days, seen a star like Elvis Presley. I've never seen so many people of all ages waiting so long outside the gates for just one glimpse of Elvis ..."

Although some of his later movies were decidedly thin on plot, according to Colonel Parker, Elvis never objected to any scripts offered to him. Explained The Colonel: "For the $500,000 a picture they're paying him, plus $5,000 a day overtime — they're going to offer Elvis a bad script?"

Friends of Elvis say he hated the later movies and refused to watch them with anyone present. So if you want to trick the King into revealing himself, don't put on a re-run of, say, the last 20-odd movies he made.

But Elvis LOVES *King Creole, Love Me Tender, Jailhouse Rock,* and *Flaming Star.* You won't go wrong starting with *King Creole,* because

Elvis turns the Jailhouse into an amazing rock stage in Jailhouse Rock, made in 1957 and condemned from the pulpit. There's plenty for Elvis fans: kissin' (with Jennifer Holden); a violent flogging; singing of several hit songs; and amazing dance scenes.

The Reno Brothers, played by Elvis and Richard Egan, in Love Me Tender, with the Debra Paget as the girl they both adored.

according to the King, that was the movie in which he did his best job of acting.

If you want to trap the King by getting his pelvis moving, try screening *Jailhouse Rock* — Elvis choreographed the title number.

When first released, *Jailhouse Rock* was banned in many towns throughout Britain after being slammed as "sex-crazed and disgusting" by British film critics. London reviewers described the film as "an unsavoury, nauseating and muddy brew of delinquency, bad taste and violence". In Australia, church leaders and psychiatrists also called for the movie to be banned.

Retorted The King in 1961: "Censorship is a joke, although I have obeyed it. The movement I did — that everyone who is supposed to know what's right objected to — was eliminated from my early movies. Now everyone is doing it, only more exaggeratedly, and they call it 'The Twist'! Some of the people I have seen doing it should not be doing it — they are vulgar."

Elvis' ambition was always "to do a Frank Sinatra" by playing a dramatic role without singing a single song. *Flaming Star* has a particular attraction for Elvis, because it gave him that chance, much to The Colonel's disgust. Elvis gives a strong performance as the half-breed son of an Indian woman and a white rancher. The movie had an unusual spin-off: it saw Elvis become an **HONORARY RED INDIAN.** He was inducted into the Los Angeles Indian Tribal Council in December 1960 by Chief Wah-nee-Ota in recognition of his performance.

On the other side of the world, in South Africa, *Flaming Star* was banned — because the western showed a white man living with an Indian woman!

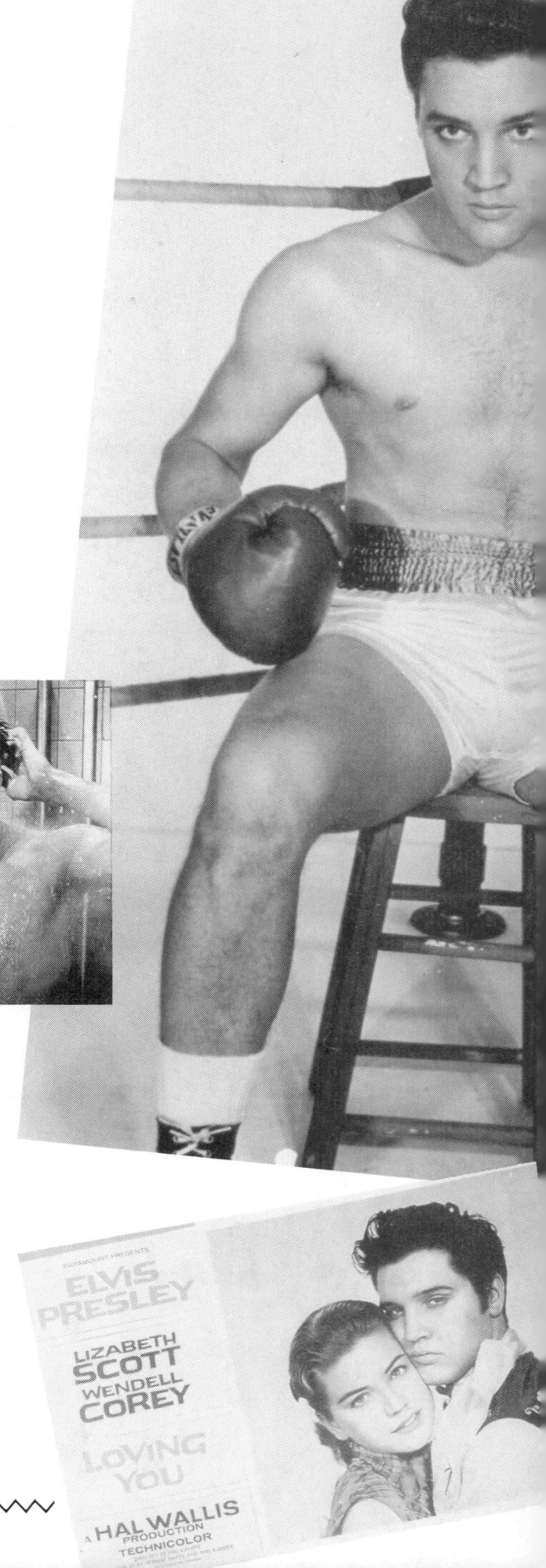

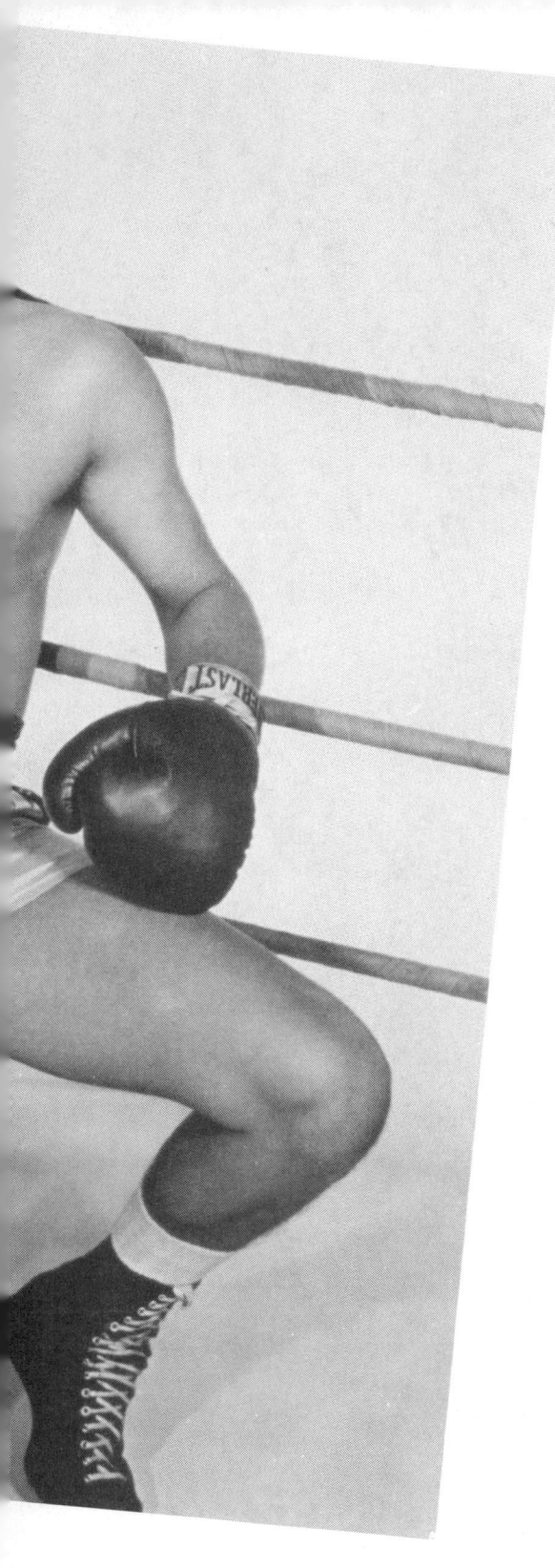

In Roustabout (1964) Elvis once again has a chance to indulge in his love for motorcycle riding, singing and the odd brawl. He hated this movie ... so don't show it if you want the King's attention.

In Girls, Girls, Girls and Loving You, the King does just that: loves lots of girls! Even his strangest expressions, like that under the shower in GI Blues (top left), had girls in ecstasy, while his muscular torso (above) knocked them out in Kid Galahad.

Apart from those few Elvis movies, you could trick the King to come out into the open by screening some of his other favourites:

✔ **Dr Strangelove:** As one of his confidants revealed, Elvis "saw Dr Strangelove three times running, from about 1:00 in the morning till 5:30; then he had the last reel repeated three times more, explaining that Peter Sellers was such a subtle actor you could not understand exactly what he was doing in just a few viewings."

✔ **Dirty Harry:** This Clint Eastwood detective drama made an enormous impression in Elvis and he watched it many times at Graceland. He took a lead from "Dirty Harry" and immediately bought a nickel-plated, long-barreled Colt .44 Magnum revolver, which he wears in a bulging shoulder holster.

✔ **Monty Python movies.**

✔ **Great fights of the Century.**

Elvis loves girls and dogs, so in Live A Little, Love A Little, the producers gave him beautiful Michelle Carey and an unnamed hound dog to keep him happy.

In Spinout (1966) Elvis played a racing driver (left) who won girls and races and more girls, while in Viva Las Vegas he romanced stunning Ann-Margret both on and off the screen.

"I was famished for brain food, so I ordered a king-size hot pepperoni pizza and told them to hold the anchovies and peppers. I opened the door and there was the King carrying the king-size hot pepperoni pizza and I knew it was him when I saw there really was no anchovies or peppers, the others always get it wrong."
— Eddie W. Isemouth, student.

ELVIS *Today?*

* Elvis loves eating pizzas and driving trucks.

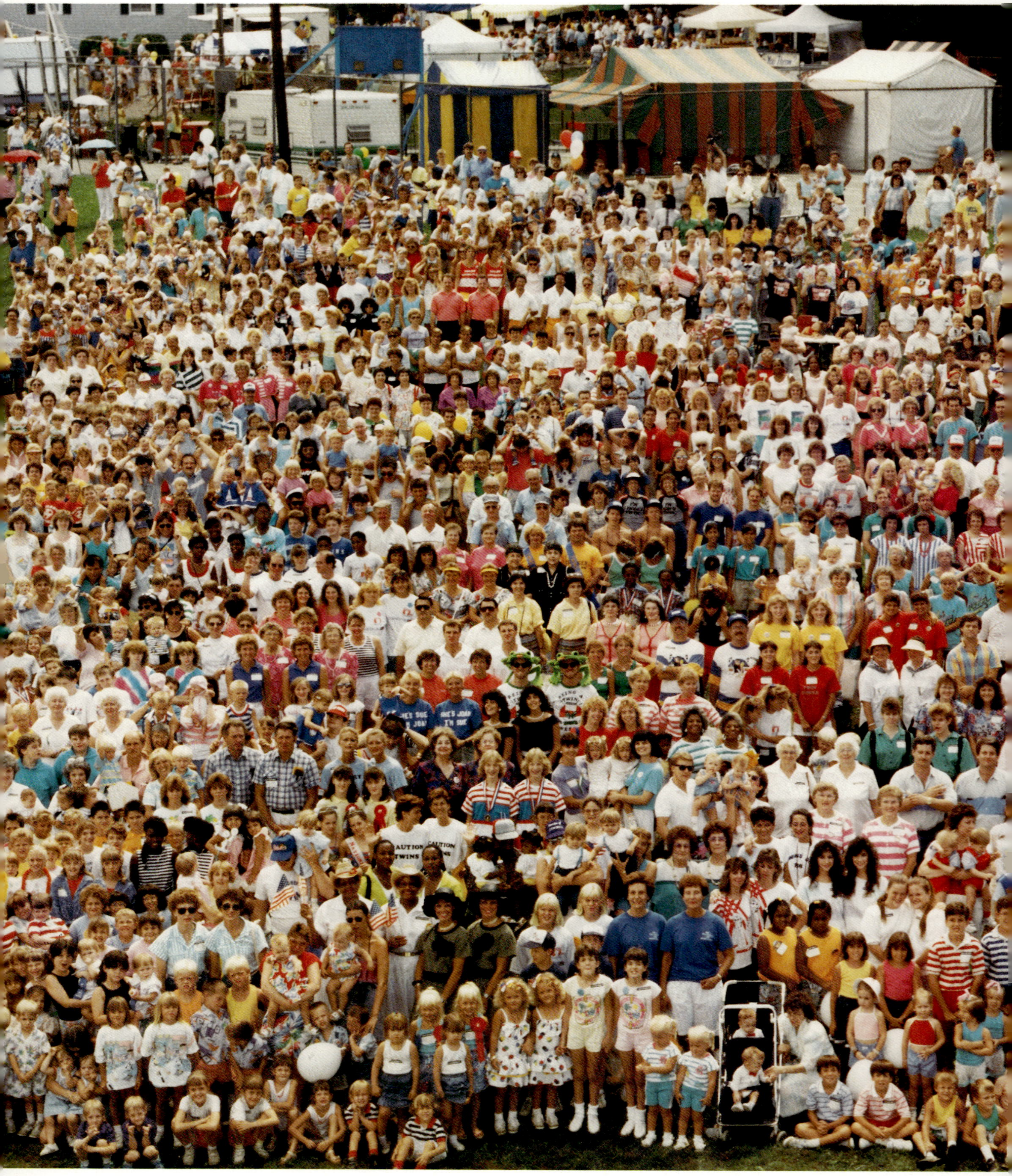

★ Is this Elvis — and his twin? Are both the Presley brothers alive?

YES, says Marcus von Smelder, who made this rare AUTHENTIC sighting of The King (and what appeared to be his twin brother Jessie Garon) when they emerged briefly from hiding to attend the world's biggest twins convention.

Held in Twinsberg, Ohio, and attracting thousands of twins from around the world, the event is enough to make anyone see double.

But, insists Mr Von Smelder (who himself bears a remarkable resemblance to the YOUNG ELVIS), he saw The King and His Twin Brother singly, or rather, together!

"They were there, clear as daylight, stuffing their faces with disgustingly big hamburgers," the internationally famous twins researcher from Duplexville, Alaska, revealed. "I know it was the Elvis brothers because at the sing-along during the convention, there were only two voices that came through with a sound that could only have come from the King.

SIGNIFICANT FACT: In his first movie, *Love Me Tender*, Elvis had a brother: the movie's original title was *The Reno Brothers*. Even more significantly, one Reno brother (played by Elvis) dies in the movie, but comes back ghostlike to sing at the end.

Mr Von Smelder insists the Presley Brothers appear somewhere in this picture, but because his eyesight is failing, he has been unable to point them out. However, he says he last saw the Presleys somewhere on the left near the centre when the group assembled for the photograph.

There have long been rumours that Elvis' twin brother, Jessie Garon, who was born first, did not actually die in childbirth, but recovered from a grave illness and was brought up by relatives because the Presleys were too poor to support two children.

Double Trouble!

ELVIS Today?

"Pull over! That's what he said! At first I wondered what this creep was pulling me over for, but then he flashed twenty, TWENTY!!, sheriff's badges at me and grinned and started to sing about 'One for the money...' and that's when I realised it was no ordinary highway patrolman ...!"

—Lennie Schwarz, banker

* Elvis' high school ambition was to become a Tennessee State Highway Patrolman. He was made an honorary captain of the Louisiana State Highway Patrol in 1956.

Is This Elvis?

★ IS THIS ELVIS? That's the question most often by the media around the world as photographers and eyewitnesses present photographs and descriptions of what they claim are genuine sightings of the King. Of course, many photos never get published because editors suspect hucksters at work. But are they right? Are there genuine pictures of Elvis that have never been published because an editor thought they were fakes?

Why don't you be the judge - and test your ability to spot a fake! On these seven pages are reproduced, exclusively for our readers, a host of photographs which are said to show Elvis since his "death". Study them carefully, then tick the relevant box to show how authentic you think each picture or picture sequence is.

Observed pumping petrol at an undisclosed location in Australia is this tubby, heavily bearded person which photographer E.P. King claims is Elvis today. King says it is highly significant that the man wore a name badge reading "Aaron" (Elvis' second name) and that he shielded his face to prevent further photography. When King enquired about the man from the cashier, she denied all knowledge of someone called Aaron working there.
If it is Elvis, he must be broke: he was not only pumping petrol, but shielded his face with a copy of a magazine called GET RICH NEWS, which bills itself "Australia's leading money ideas magazine". Significantly, a major story in the magazine tells how to cash in on videos.

GENUINENESS RATING:
☐ Certain
☐ Probable
☐ Possible
☐ Unlikely
☐ Fake

When Bette Wilson realised the person sitting next to her at Circular Quay railway station in Sydney, Australia, was almost certainly Elvis, she asked a friend to pretend to take a photo of her clowning around - but to make sure Elvis was secretly included. But the King must have become suspicious, for immediately after the photo was taken in early 1992, he ran off into the night.

GENUINENESS RATING:

☐ Certain

☐ Probable

☐ Possible

☐ Unlikely

☐ Fake

This exclusive photograph, claimed to have been taken recently at a high-level centre for undercover narcotics agents somewhere in the USA, could be the best proof offered yet that the King underwent plastic surgery to escape from the Mafia and continue his relentless fight against crime. (For an artist's impression, see Page 57). Faces of others in the photo have been disguised to protect them from assassination.

GENUINENESS RATING:

☐ Certain

☐ Probable

☐ Possible

☐ Unlikely

☐ Fake

Did Elvis suffer horrible disfigurement in a petrol-bomb attack while he was working undercover as a narc? Did the searing heat melt his face to such an extent that even the world's best plastic surgeons could only reconstruct it into what appears to be a deathly white mask? Did the King go into hiding in a very secret tropical sanctuary, complete with a private golf course and guarded by fierce dogs, near the infamous Golden Triangle in Thailand?

Those are the claims made by a Swedish freelance photographer who says he found Elvis playing golf at his hideaway in the tropical north of Thailand and snatched these exclusive photographs. He claims Elvis' obvious affection for a brown hound dog, which followed him about everywhere, is further proof that this is the King.

FAKE? FUNSTER? OR FOR REAL?

GENUINENESS RATING:
☐ Certain
☐ Probable
☐ Possible
☐ Unlikely
☐ Fake

Is this the Son of Elvis? The photograph, sent exclusively to the pop music editor of a popular newspaper in La Paz, Bolivia, had a note attached which read "El Bambino". There must be some doubt about its authenticity, however, because it is unusual for such young children to have such luxuriant sideburns.

45

"I AIN'T NOTHIN' BUT A ... ??"

⭐ Did Elvis employ plastic surgery to change his appearance after his reported "death"? And, if the King has altered his appearance so radically, how could you recognise him in the street?
As an exclusive guide to readers of THE ELVIS SPOTTER'S GUIDE, we have had a top Identikit expert reconstruct his appearance based on descriptions from his most likely recent sightings, using the same face (the way he looked in *Jailhouse Rock*) as a basis for the reconstruction.

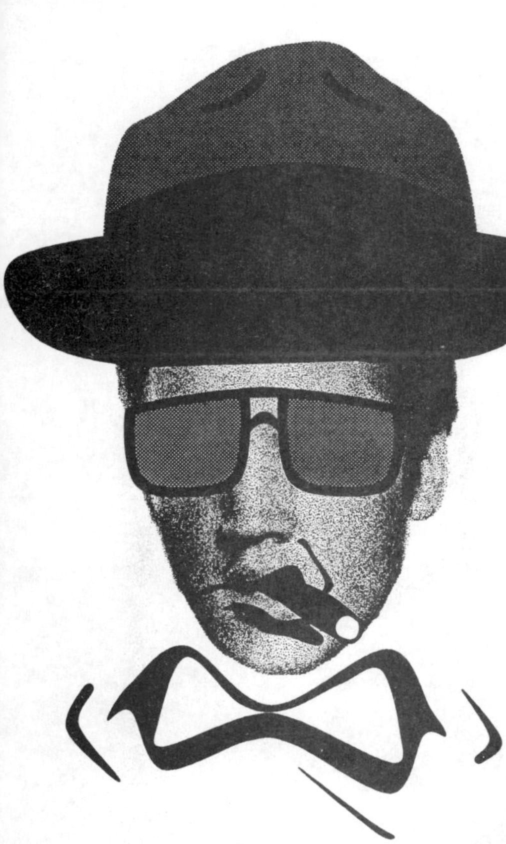

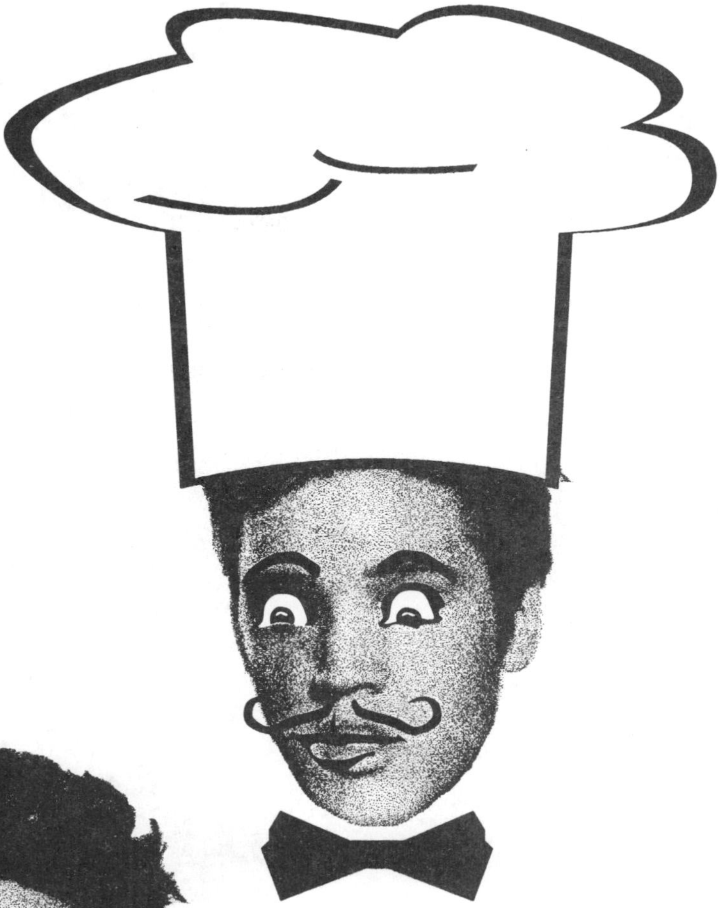

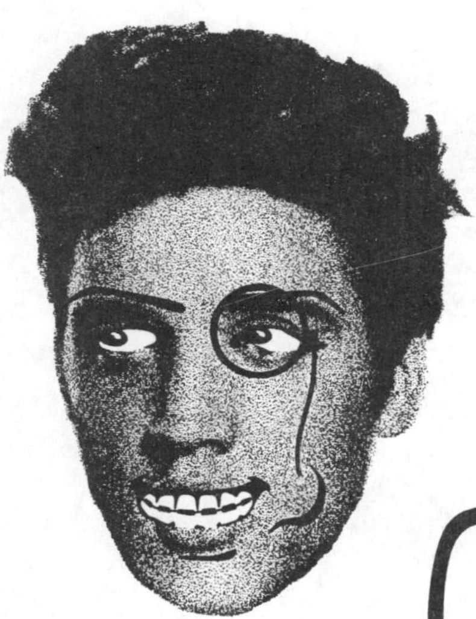

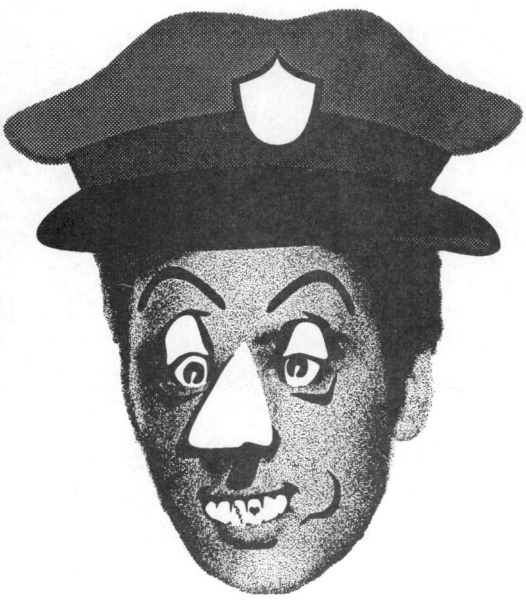

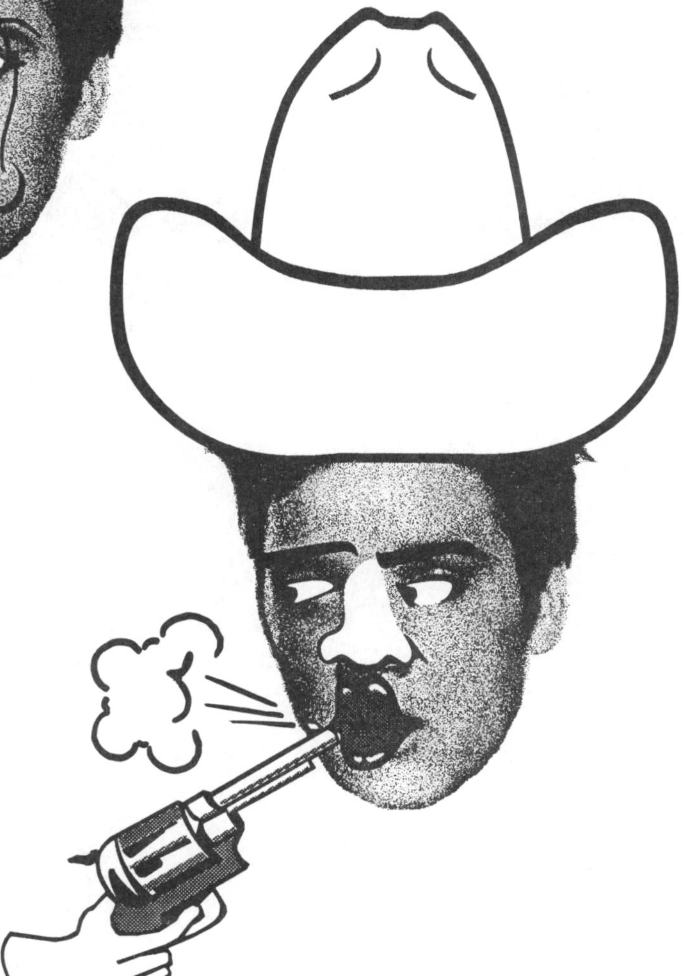

The Many Faces of Elvis!

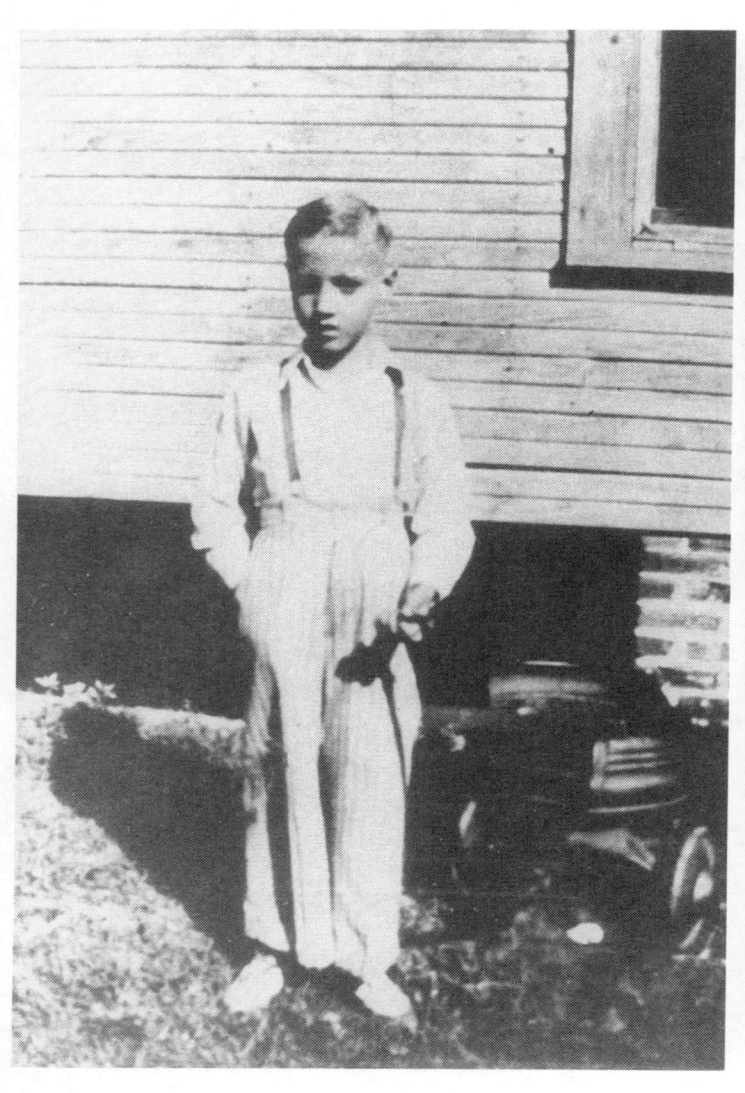

Portraits of The King ... Elvis as a child who grew up to be the world's greatest rock artist. Left: Country boy Elvis in his hit movie Love Me Tender that took the world by storm.

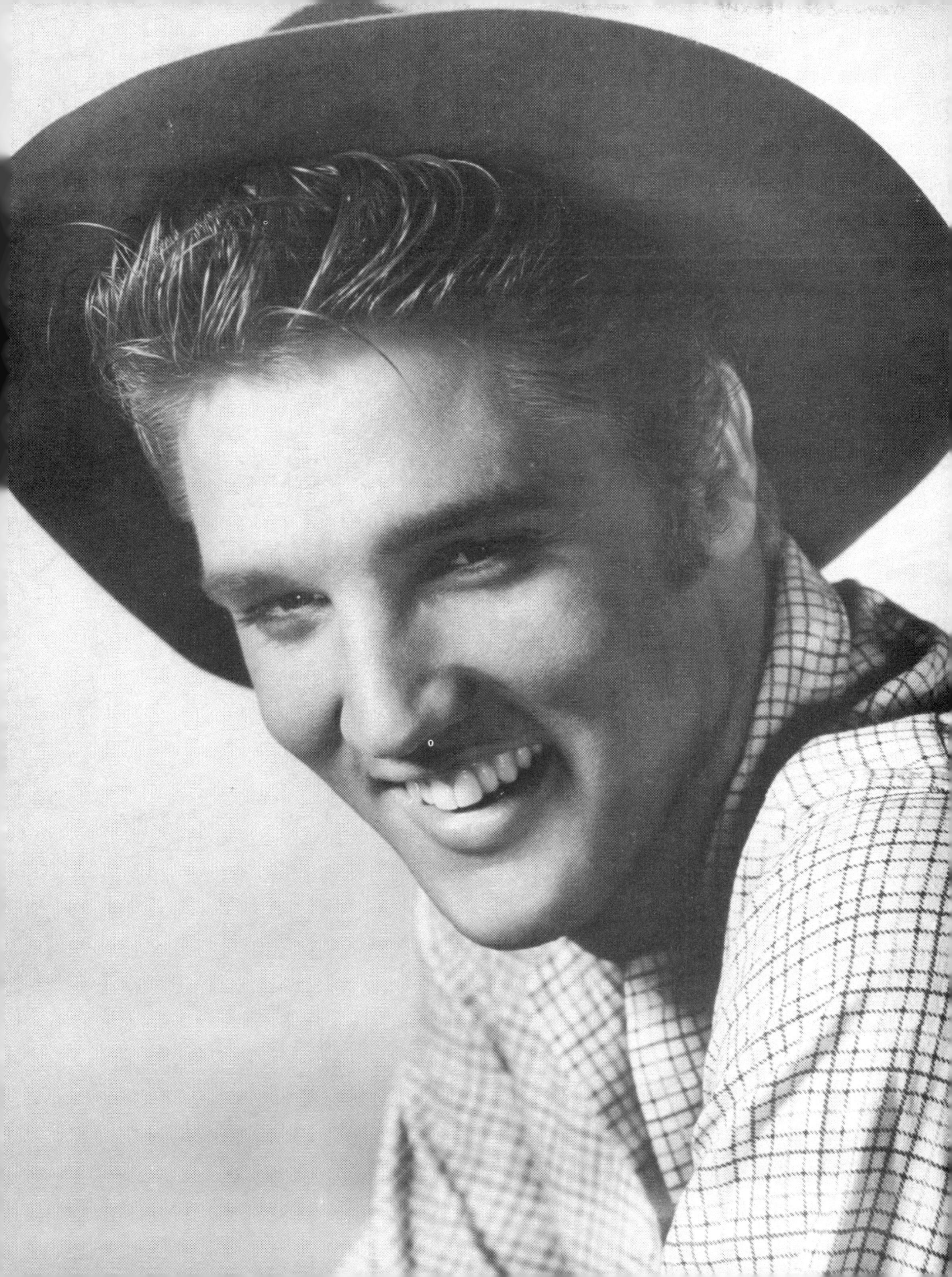

Uncle Sam wants YOU, said the poster .. so the King of Rock went with a smile. It cost him his hair (left) and that saddened millions of female fans, but his good conduct won Elvis an honourable discharge (above).

Rock-'n-Roll Presley style ... it was performances like these that made Elvis the King at an early age.

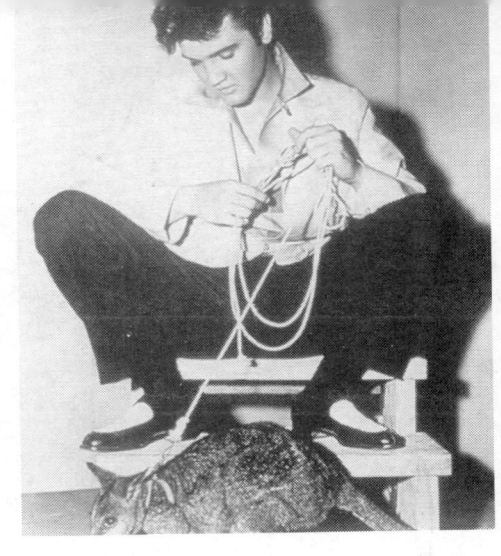

Hollywood Hound! Left: Elvis previews his movie screen test with producer Hal Wallis. Above: Relaxing between scenes while filming Jailhouse Rock. Below: The King in pensive mood during filming.

The Elvis Spotter's Quiz

To track down and identify Elvis, you'll need an excellent knowledge of his life and work. Here's a 100-question quiz about the King that will test your knowledge about a wide range of Presleyana. All the answers are in *The Elvis Spotter's Guide*, so if you've done your homework, you should pass with distinction. (Turn to Page 96 if you're really stumped.)

1. Of whom did Elvis say in August 1959: "She looks like an angel"?

2. What fear did Elvis believe witnessing autopsies would overcome?

3. How many movies did Elvis make during his career?

4. In which Elvis movie does his parents appear very briefly in a crowd scene?

5. Elvis collects the records of which famous opera tenor?

6. To loosen his vocal chords before going on stage, Elvis always has a large mug of tea laced with what?

7. From which movie does Elvis' musical theme tune *Also Sprach Zarathustra* come?

8. Elvis designed a logo for his staff consisting of the letters TCB with a gold thunderbolt crashing through them. What do the letters stand for?

9. With his very first royalty cheque, Elvis bought his mother what present?

10. What was the name of Elvis' pet male chow on which he spent a fortune for treatment for near-fatal kidney failure in 1975?

11. What unusual outfit did Colonel Parker wear to Elvis' funeral?

12. How old was Elvis when he bought Graceland?

13. Which communist country declared Elvis "Public Enemy No. 1" of its teenagers in November 1959?

14. What was the name of Elvis' private jet?

15. On 7 July 1954 Dewey Phillips became the first disc jockey to play an Elvis Presley record on the radio, on station WHBQ in which city in the U.S.A.?

16. In what movie, released on 6 March 1964, did Elvis play two roles, one of them in a blond wig?

(was a hillbilly named Jodie Tatum)?

17. What was the title of Elvis' first commercial record release?

18. On 8 September 1979, a huge bronze statue of Elvis was unveiled in the lobby of which famous Las Vegas Hotel?

19. Lisa Marie's middle name was in honour of the wife of which close associate of Elvis?

20. What year did Elvis enter the US Army?

21. What 1942 model car did Vernon Presley buy for $50 for Elvis as an 18th birthday present?

22. Elvis' first album after being released from the army was not *G.I. Blues,* but _____?

23. As a young boy, Elvis' favourite comic book hero was Captain ____?

24. Elvis wore jeans in only one movie. Which one was it?

25. Which single, released on 27 January 1956, sold a million copies in one week, giving Elvis his first nationwide hit in the USA?

26. Elvis' serial number in the army was 53310761, preceded by two letters. What were they?

27. Elvis' first full-time job was driving a truck for which Memphis company?

28. What speech defect of Elvis was shown in the movies *Kissin' Cousins* and *Wild in the Country*?

29. Which pop star was once arrested for crashing though the gates at Graceland at 3 o'clock in the morning carrying a pistol and daring Elvis to come out?

30. Which famous movie star's life did Elvis want to portray on screen "more than anything else"?

31. Lisa Marie Presley was born on 1 February of which year?

32. What farm animals did Elvis' mother keep at Graceland?

33. In which 1965 movie did Elvis dress up as an Arab?

34. How much did Elvis pay for Graceland?

35. Elvis made three movies with the word *Girls* in the title. They were ____?

36. What is the address for Graceland?

37. What did Elvis drink on his 40th birthday?

38. What lifetime fear did Elvis have to overcome for the movie *Blue Hawaii*?

39. What four-wheel vehicle did Elvis race around Graceland?

40. What did Lisa Marie weigh when she was born?

41. In which Las Vegas hotel did Elvis and Priscilla hold their wedding reception?

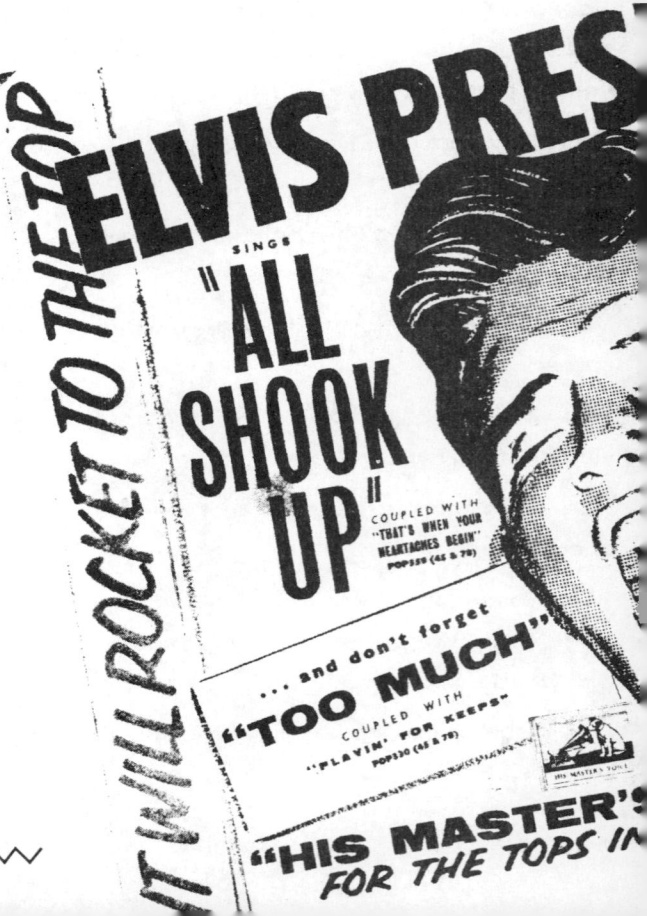

42. How many pairs of pants does Elvis buy with every suit?

43. What was the flip side of the Elvis hit *Hound Dog*, recorded on 2 July 1956?

44. What colour are Elvis' eyes?

45. Until her confinement when Elvis was born, his mother Gladys worked as what?

46. What did Elvis give Priscilla for her graduation present?

47. What was the title of Elvis' first movie?

48. On the memorial to his mother at Forest Hills Cemetery, what did Elvis have inscribed?

49. The call-sign for Elvis' Convair 880 plane was what?

50. What is the name of Elvis' grand-daughter?

51. Whose portraits did Elvis have on either side of his bed at Graceland?

52. In which movie did Elvis play the role of Clint Reno?

53. Elvis' favourite ice-creams are ____?

54. Elvis brushes his teeth several times a day with what brand of toothpaste?

55. How old was Elvis when he married Priscilla?

56. Elvis wore a beard in only one movie. Can you name it?

57. What make is Elvis' favourite motorcycle?

58. What size shoe does Elvis wear?

59. Under what star sign was Elvis born?

60. Elvis was inducted into the Los Angeles Indian Tribal Council in December 1960 by Chief Wah-nee-Ota in recognition of his performance in which movie?

61. What are the colours of the enamel shield that Elvis received when he was appointed by President Nixon as a narcotics agent?

62. What is the missing word in the following Elvis movie title: *Follow That _____*?

63. Who was Elvis' leading lady in his last film, *Change Of Habit*?

64. What is Elvis' favourite passage in the Bible?

65. What is Elvis' nickname for his mother, Gladys?

66. What is Elvis' favourite sport?

67. In which year did Elvis leave high school?

68. What was the name of Elvis' Palamino horse which he kept at his Circle G Ranch?

69. What is the missing word in the following Elvis movie title: *_____ Hawaiian Style*.

70. When Priscilla and Elvis were married, she promised to "love, honour and _____?

71. Elvis married Priscilla in Las Vegas on 1 May of which year?

72. Which movie producer, after screen testing Elvis in April 1956 and signing him to a $450,000 deal to make three films over seven years, said: "I had the same thrill on seeing Error Flynn for the first time"?

73. Elvis' antique Carl Hauptmann-Ferlach double-barrelled hunting rifle once belonged to which famous Nazi?

74. To whom did Elvis get engaged on 26 January 1977, after consulting *Cheiro's Book of Numbers*?

75. What school sports team was Elvis thrown out of because he ignored instructions from the coach to get his hair cut?

76. In which movie did Elvis play a Southern country singer named Deke Rivers?

77. What is Elvis' favourite board game, which he spent the evening of his 40th birthday playing?

78. What was the name of Priscilla's horse at the Circle G Ranch?

79. If Elvis and Priscilla had a boy, what name did they plan to give him?

80. What pseudonym did Elvis use in his note to President Nixon?

81. In which movie did Elvis first dye his hair from his natural light-brown to a darker shade?

82. In the autumn of 1956, Elvis was made an honorary captain of which State Highway Patrol?

83. What rank did Elvis have when he was released from the Army on 5 March 1960?

84. Elvis' first record was *That's Alright, Mama*. What was the flip side?

85. Of which co-star in the movie *Speedway* did Elvis say: "She's difficult to get along with, but she's my kinda gal"?

86. What is Priscilla's pet name for Elvis?

87. What important role did Dr. William R. Hunt of Mississippi play in the life of Elvis?

88. Which female movie star did Elvis want to visit in Paris while serving in the army in Europe?

89. What was Elvis' nickname for himself in the 1960s?

90. Which famous comedian paid $22,000 for two pairs of leather trousers which once belonged to Elvis - and then had them altered so he could wear them himself?

91. What is Elvis' nickname for Priscilla?

92. Which Elvis movie was banned in South Africa because Presley played the son of a white man and an Indian woman?

93. What operation did Elvis have on 18 June 1975 at the Mid-South Hospital in Memphis?

94. Which university in the U.S.A. offers a course entitled, *The Cultural Phenomenon of Elvis Presley: The Making of a Folk Hero*?

95. What was Elvis' job in the army?

96. What weapon does Elvis carry in his boot when he goes on stage?

97. What is the name of the high school Elvis attended?

98. Elvis' mother was born on 25 April 1912 in Pototuc County, Mississippi, one of 10 children. What was her full maiden name?

99. What childish word does Elvis use for feet in love talk?

100. What was the name of Elvis' first steady girlfriend, whom he dated at the age of 15?

ELVIS Today?

"When E.P. first asked to join us, it was natural that he would become a Special Operative in our narcotics division because of his encyclopaedic knowledge of drugs and drug laws. But he kept on bursting into song while on the job, so we had to post him abroad disguised as Elvis Presley."
- Assistant Associate Deputy Director (U.S.N.B.) Joseph Needlemeir.

* President Nixon appointed Elvis an agent of the Bureau of Narcotics

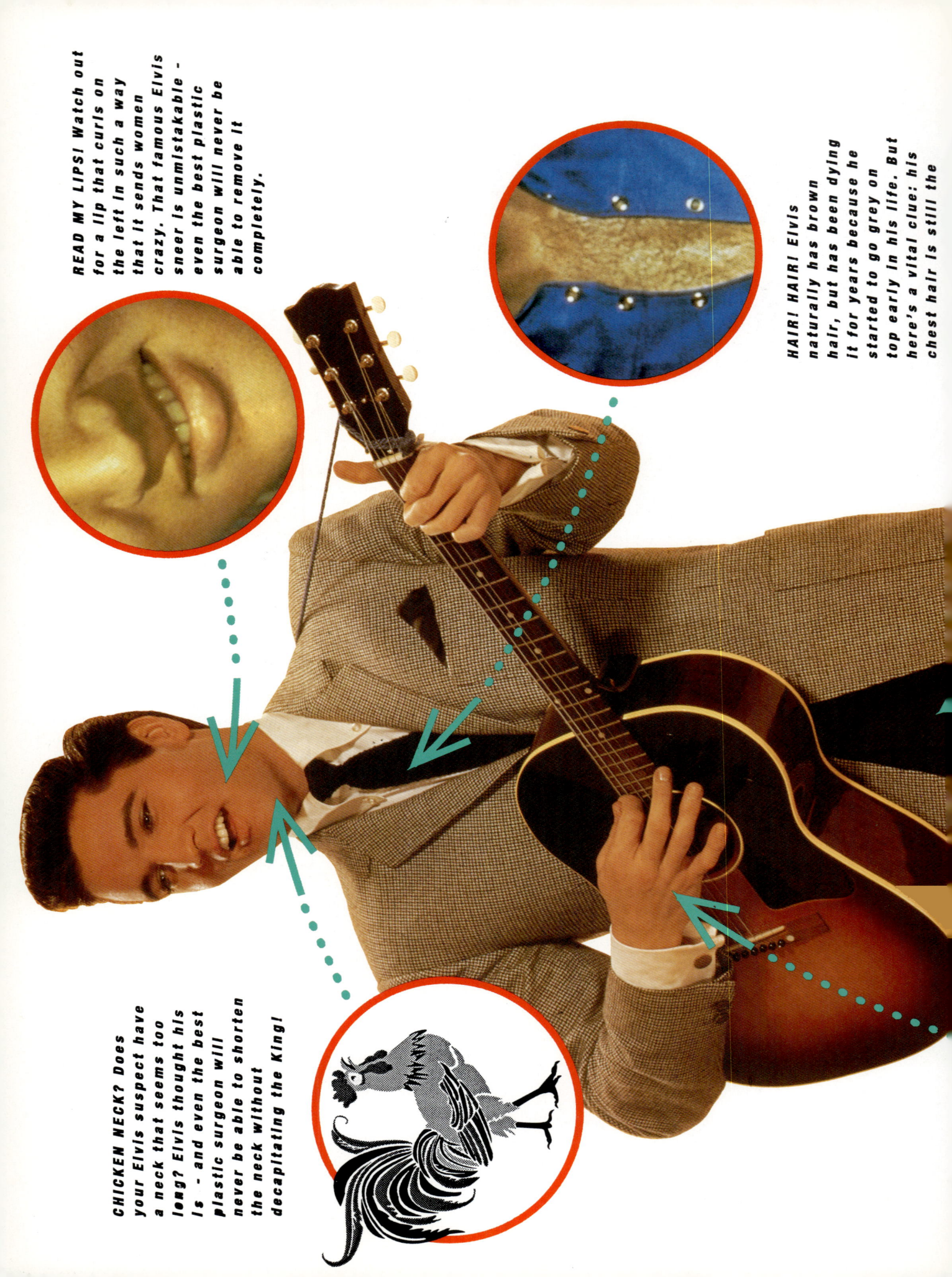

READ MY LIPS! Watch out for a lip that curls on the left in such a way that it sends women crazy. That famous Elvis sneer is unmistakable – even the best plastic surgeon will never be able to remove it completely.

HAIR! HAIR! Elvis naturally has brown hair, but has been dying it for years because he started to go grey on top early in his life. But here's a vital clue: his chest hair is still the

CHICKEN NECK? Does your Elvis suspect have a neck that seems too long? Elvis thought his is – and even the best plastic surgeon will never be able to shorten the neck without decapitating the King!

Elvis Identifier!

ELVIS THE PELVIS! The King can't help gyrating those famous hips that have driven millions of females into a frenzy - so watch out for the tell-tale signs. But DON'T call him "Elvis the Pelvis" - he'll think you're being childish.

HANDY HINT: Karate scars, a fractured fifth finger of his right hand and rings including a diamond horseshoe, a diamond-studded wedding band and a red ruby karate ring are sure clues to the King's identity.

ELVIS Today?

"Uncle Ernie was my life, but when I saw it was Elvis who had assisted at the autopsy, then I knew he was in the hands of an Angel!"
- Masie Aronski, grandmother

* Elvis visits morgues and attends autopsies to overcome his fear of blood.

HERE I AM! The Elvis Ready Reckoner

★ Elvis often wore disguises - ranging from wigs to masks - even while living at Graceland and also changed his appearance by dying his hair, having a face-lift and using a variety of make-up tricks.

Gail Brewer-Giorgio, Elvis expert and author of the best-selling book *Is Elvis Alive?*, stresses that he loved masks and disguises. A 1976 newspaper report reveals he often used a blond wig as a disguise to fool fans, while another close source says that when driving around Memphis, "to avoid attention ... he would put a disguising cap on his head and go out for a ... cruise in a panel truck that had been used to haul garbage off the property at Graceland".

You might even find Elvis masquerading today as a wealthy Sheik: after all, he liked his Arab costume in *Harum Scarum* so much he used to wear it home to dinner in Graceland each night after shooting finished! In fact, the King was so fascinated by Rudolf Valentino's hold over women that in *Harum Scarum* he tried to look as much as Valentino did in his most famous movie, *The Sheik*, down to duplicating the silent movie idol's heavy, dark make-up.

To track down and identify the King, you'll obviously need to know much more than just what his photos show. You'll need the best possible artist's impressions of what he might look like today (our colour recreations should prove an invaluable aid), but also what hard-to-disguise physical characteristics and habits to be on the look-out for. Here's your **ELVIS READY RECKONER**, to be used in conjunction with the Easy Elvis Identifier on pages 58 and 59.

ARMPIT: Elvis uses Brut deodorant. If you can't get close enough to smell his armpit, look for a tell-tale bulge made by the King's shoulder holster which usually holds a nickel-plated, long-barrelled Colt .44 magnum revolver. To see what it looks like, rent a copy of the Clint Eastwood movie *Dirty Harry* - that's what inspired Elvis to get his magnum!

BEARD: Elvis' beard is dark brown, as you can see in the movie *Charro*. The King likes a close shave, using a Wilkinson straight razor, but sometimes he is lazy and settles for an electric shaver.

BIRTHMARK: Elvis has a heart-shaped birthmark on his front hairline, caused when he was forcibly extracted from his mother's womb by Dr William R. Hunt on 8 January 1935.

CHEEK: Ask your Elvis suspect for an autograph - and if his right cheek twitches, you've found the King!

COMPLEXION: Elvis regularly applies facial creams designed to keep the skin smooth to his face, especially if he notes the slightest sign of a wrinkle. FBI files reveal that in 1959 a South African dermatologist was hired by Elvis to treat wrinkles on his forehead, crowsfeet at his eyes and other minor skin blemishes on his face and shoulders; Laurens Johannes Griessel-Landau repaid the King by attempting to blackmail him over Elvis' relationship with Priscilla, who was then only 16 years old.

EYEBROWS: Elvis' eyebrows and eyelashes started to turn grey in his early thirties, when he started dying them black.

EYES: Elvis' eyes are blue/hazel.

FACE-LIFT: Elvis had a face-lift at the Mid-South Hospital in Memphis on 18 June 1975.

FEET: Elvis always wears US size 11D footwear, all of which (from shoes to boots to bedroom slippers) have a half-inch lift and an inch or one-and-a-half-inch heel. His boots are black, blue or white patent leather Verdis or San Remos. If you can get close enough, check for a Berringer pistol in his boot.

FINGER: Elvis fractured his fifth finger of his right hand while playing football. He was hospitalised for this from 16 to 17 August 1960 at the Baptist Memorial Hospital in Memphis. Two months later he recorded *I Slipped, I Stumbled, I Fell*.

HAIR: Elvis' naturally brown hair was already thickly streaked with grey by the time he reached his early thirties. The King uses *Prell Shampoo for Dyed Hair* and a hairspray called *Presto*.

HAIRLINE: Look out for tiny marks on the scalp at the hairline - that could be the vital give-away! The reason? The King regularly applies tiny dots with an eyebrow pencil so he can monitor any sign of the hairline receding.

HANDS: Look out for the heavily calloused hands of a karate black belt. Elvis dedicated himself to this martial-arts hobby for over 18 years, after first becoming interested while in the army in Germany. He holds an eighth-degree black belt. "It's an art, not a sport," the King declared. "It involved the Buddhist monks. They had no way of protecting themselves from robbers. So they studied the different animals. They studied the tiger..."

HEIGHT: Elvis is five feet eleven inches (180cm) tall.

JEWELLERY: Elvis likes certain items of jewellery so much he may well be wearing replicas of them today. These include a kenpo karate ring with a big red ruby, a diamond horseshoe-shaped ring, and a diamond-studded wrist watch, similar to that presented to him by RCA in 1961 for selling 76 million records. In his last years at Graceland he also habitually wore a Star of David around his neck.

LEGS: Elvis referrs to his legs as "gantlin'" and hated exposing them in beach movies.

MOUTH: Check for that famous lip that curls up on the left. And when Elvis drinks from his cup, reveals one expert source, "he will twist it around so his lips touch the rim above the handle, a part never soiled by contact with another person's lips".

NECK: Elvis wears high collars, but the exact reason is not certain. Some close associates claim it is because he believes his neck is too long and that the collars disguise this "chicken" neck. But according to Larry Geller, Elvis' hairdresser and spiritual "guru", the King wore high collars because he had been inspired by drawings of various spiritual masters wearing high collars in one of his favourite books, *Through the Eyes of the Masters* by David Andreas. Elvis also has some acne scars on the back of his neck and on a few places on his chin.

SMELL: Elvis prefers *Neutragena* soap (although Priscilla complained that he rarely bathes) and masks any odours by spraying himself with Brut. Biographer Arthur Goldman, drawing on inside information from former Memphis Mafia member Lamar Fike, notes that "Priscilla was so disgusted by Elvis' lack of personal cleanliness that when she renovated their last house on Monovale Road, she had his shower stall rigged with 3 spray nozzles: one for the head, one for the torso and one for the lower extremities. It was a good idea but Elvis objected".

SOCKS: Elvis wears calf-length socks in matching colours; red is a favourite.

TEETH: Elvis has always hated the gap between his front teeth. He had it capped at the age of 18 - which is why there are no photographs extant showing him smiling before then. He carries a spare tooth cap with him at all times, even when he goes on stage. The King brushes his teeth several times a day with *Colgate*.

VOICE: Of course, that incredible voice would be very difficult to disguise, so the surest way to check out an Elvis suspect would be to get him to sing one of the King's more difficult songs, like *Heartbreak Hotel* or *Hound Dog*. Another, and much more subtle, give-away to look for when your Elvis suspect is speaking, is a slight stutter. This began in Junior High School in Memphis; Elvis once told how this speech defect resulted in "the kids ... inviting me to parties so they could make fun of me". Elvis stutters whenever he talks rapidly or is nervous. *SPOTTING TIP:* Check out the stutter by watching repeatedly the relevant scenes in two movies: *Kissin' Cousins* and, for a more pronounced stutter, a drinking scene in *Wild in the Country*.

Amazing Elvis!

300 FACTS TO GET YOU ALL SHOOK UP

1. During the opening scenes of the movie *Elvis: On Tour*, the King relates his father's warning to him when he made his first record. Vernon had said: "Son, you better make up your mind whether you want to be a guitar player or an electrician - because I never saw a guitar player that was worth a damn..."

2. "When he's away on tour he phones home every night and says, 'How are my babies?' I call him Baby or Ageless. That's because when he was little, his cousin couldn't say Elvis." - Gladys Presley in 1955.

3. Elvis about his mother: "When she yelled at me, I thought she hated me, but now I know she was only doing it for my own good."

4. Elvis always carries a spare tooth cap because he hates the gap between his front teeth which he had capped at the age of 18.

5. Elvis always carries a hand-gun, usually a .38 Magnum, but aides ensure the first chamber is empty to prevent accidents.

6. The King in May 1956: "His brown hair doesn't appear so dark, either. He has pimples all over the back of his neck, a few on his chin, and a number of nervous facial mannerisms. The most intriguing is the repeated, rapid puffing of a single cheek. His long eyelashes have a Valentine-like mascaraed look. ... His right cheek twitched each time he signed an autograph." - *Minneapolis Globe*.

7. The mother of Elvis' fiancee, Ginger Alden, claimed in 1978 that she had seen the King's "ghost".

8. The Presley family never paid Dr. William R. Hunt his $15 fee for delivering Elvis and his stillborn brother, Jesse Garon.

9. Elvis announced he was filing for divorce on 9 August 1972.

10. The King attends autopsies to overcome his fear of blood.

11. Elvis does not drink alcohol and even spent his 40th birthday drinking diet soft drinks.

12. 80,000 mourners passed by the coffin when "Elvis" lay in state at Graceland on 17 August 1977.

13. Elvis enjoys sitting in the driving seat of a bulldozer and smashing down old buildings.

14. Elvis enjoys reading in the bathroom.

15. A fan recently bought a pair of Elvis' underpants for $7000.

16. A Gallup Poll once showed that Elvis Presley had won more recognition with his first name than any other full name in the world.

17. A London newspaper report in May 1958 said researchers claimed that Elvis Presley fans received lower school marks than the fans of singers Pat Boone, Perry Como and Frank Sinatra. "The youth organisation that has been investigating young fans adds that Presley's admirers do not seem to be keen on joining clubs or churches - and few of them are concerned about the future."

18. A major US newspaper reported in 1958 that during his first few nights in an army bunk, Elvis slept with his teddy bear clutched close. "The incident caused such a furore around the camp, that the commanding officer had to order Elvis to do away with his fuzzy friend," added the report.

19. A man repeatedly telephoned Graceland in 1968, claiming Elvis had been killed in a plane crash in Kentucky, his FBI file reveals.

20. A Memphis Mafia member about Priscilla: "She looked like she had about eight people living in her hair."

21. Elvis' ex-girlfriend Linda Thompson is a former Miss Tennessee.

22. According to Marty Lecker, one of the Memphis Mafia, Elvis always kept at least a million dollars in his cheque account just in case he wanted to write out a cheque to buy something.

23. Elvis first became interested in karate while in the army in Germany.

24. When country star Red Sovine recorded *Teddy Bear* - a different song from Elvis' 1957 hit - Colonel Tom Parker tried to sue, but without success because the court ruled there is no copyright on the title of a song.

25. When Elvis "died" he had recorded 127 gold disks - more than any other singer in history.

26. Elvis fondly nicknamed his mother, Gladys, "Satnin'".

27. "At the moment you have a million dollars worth of talent, but after I'm through with you, you'll have a million dollars." - Colonel Tom Parker to Elvis on signing a contract to manage him.

28. According to columnist Jack Anderson, when Elvis was appointed a US Federal narcotics agent, "the emotional Presley was so overwhelmed

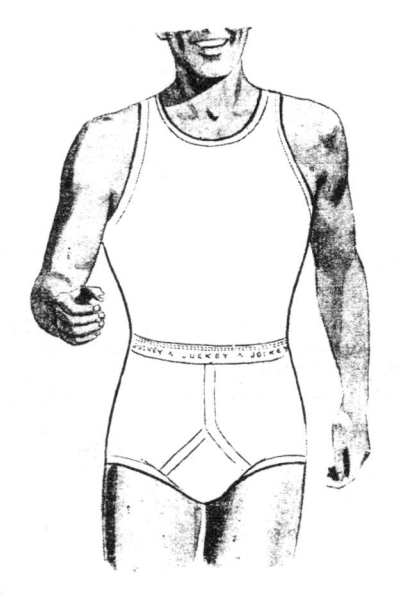

at getting his own genuine, gold-plated badge that tears sprang from his eyes and he grabbed President Nixon in a Hollywood bear hug".

29. After Linda left, Elvis (who had always been interested in death) began going to mortuaries and actually practised embalming. According to Billy Stanley, his stepbrother, "He called death the best thing that could happen to you."

30. Elvis gave Priscilla a $1-million Hollywood home as a wedding present.

31. After screen testing Elvis in April 1956 and signing him to a $450,000 deal to make three films over seven years, producer Hal Wallis enthused: "I had the same thrill on seeing Error Flynn for the first time."

32. Elvis gets very annoyed when anyone speaks to him in the morning before he has had his second cup of coffee.

33. Elvis had 16 TV sets scattered throughout Graceland. There was one in each room, two in the kitchen and three in the basement. He had two sets imbedded in the ceiling above his huge bed.

34. When *Heartbreak Hotel* was released on 27 January 1956, it sold a million copies in the first week.

35. Elvis had a gold belt buckle shaped like his deputy sheriff's star and encrusted with diamonds.

36. Elvis has a heart-shaped birthmark on his front hairline.

37. Elvis had a fear of the ocean which he had to overcome for the beach movie *Blue Hawaii*.

38. A huge bronze statue of Elvis - thought to be the world's biggest - was unveiled in the lobby of the Las Vegas Hilton Hotel on 8 September 1979.

39. Elvis had a sepia portrait of Jesus and a photo of his mother on either side of his bed in Graceland.

40. Elvis had his first professional recording session with Sun Records on 5 July 1954.

41. There were important supporters for Elvis in his home-town long before he became a national recording star. Noted a critic in the Memphis *Press-Scimitar* in 1955: "Elvis' clothes are strictly sharp. His eyes are darkly slumbrous, his hair sleekly long, his sideburns low, and there is a lazy, sexy, tough, good-looking manner which bobby soxers like. Not all record stars go over as well on stage as they do on records. Elvis sells. If the merry-go-round doesn't start spinning too fast for a 20-year-old, he'll end-up with enough cheeseburgers to last a Blue Moon."

42. Elvis has a habit of ordering two pairs of trousers with every suit -

because early in his career he often split and tore his trousers while performing.

43. Elvis has sold more records than any other singer.

44. The King hates the expression "Elvis the Pelvis". Shortly after the term was first used, he said: "I mean, it's one of the most childish expressions I have ever heard coming from an adult."

45. Elvis hates alcohol because he believes it killed his mother.

46. Elvis holds an eighth-degree black belt in karate.

47. Elvis hired a dermatologist in 1959 to treat crowsfeet and other skin blemishes on his face and shoulders.

48. "I was never too smart readin' books," Elvis confessed in a 1971 interview about his childhood. "One of the few we had at our house was *How To Win Friends And Influence People* by Dale Carnegie, which turned out to be one of the best things that happened to me. I went back to it for years when I had a problem. If you believe that book, and everyone will who reads it, we're all trying to do something in life to make ourselves feel more important."

49. Elvis is a Capricorn.

50. At their wedding, Priscilla undertook to "love, honour and comfort" Elvis.

51. Before going on stage, Elvis always has a large mug of tea laced with lots of honey to loosen his vocal cords.

52. Elvis is very religious. "He felt he had been given this gift, this talent, by God," Natalie Wood recalls. "He didn't take it for granted. He thought it was something that he had to protect. He had to be nice to people, otherwise God would take it all away."

53. Elvis left high school in 1953.

54. Before Elvis was born, his mother worked as a sewing-machine operator.

55. Elvis likes his breakfast coffee piping hot and extra strong.

56. Elvis likes to underline passages he enjoys in the Bible.

57. Elvis lost his hair to an army barber on 24 March 1961.

58. *Billboard* magazine voted Elvis the "Most Promising New Artist of the Year" in September 1954, saying he was a performer "who can sock out a tune for the country or the rhythm and blues market".

59. Strangely, Colonel Tom Parker, on hearing of Elvis' "death", said: "Nothing has changed. This won't change anything."

60. Elvis loves motorcycle racing on his Harley Davidson - and stunt riding at that! Notes one biographer: "As he and Lamar Fike would roar down

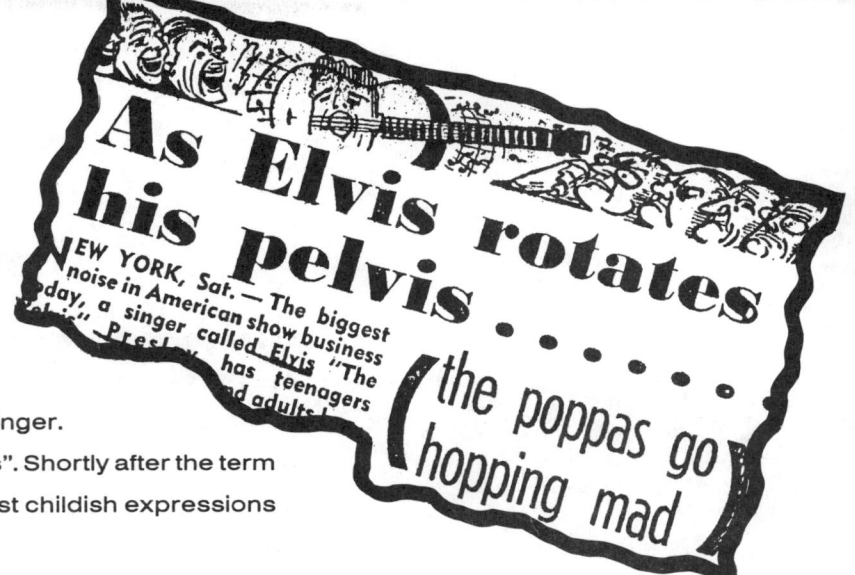

As Elvis rotates his pelvis..... the poppas go hopping mad

NEW YORK, Sat. — The biggest noise in American show business today, a singer called Elvis "The Pelvis" Presley, has teenagers and adults...

In case you want to check if Elvis has come home, the telephone number for Graceland is (901) 332-3322.

What?

Elvis once had a turkey named Bow Tie.

the empty highway, they would pull up beside each other, adjust their positions and then reach out - and touch hands at 120 m.p.h."

61. Elvis likes dressing up as an Arab sheikh - he even wore his costume in *Harum Scarum* home to Graceland after each day's filming.

62. Comedian Eddie Murphy paid $22,000 for two pairs of leather trousers which once belonged to Elvis - and then had a tailor alter them so he could wear them.

63. Elvis loves terror movies and detective thrillers.

64. Communist East Germany declared Elvis "Public Enemy No. 1" of its country's teenagers in November 1959. A newspaper said: "Schoolteachers have been ordered to report children who listen to Presley broadcasts and play forbidden Presley records."

65. During his Army service, Elvis received an estimated 15,000 letters a week from his admirers. That Christmas he received 400,000 cards from well-wishers who wanted him to know he hadn't been forgotten.

66. Elvis made 31 movies and two documentaries in his known career.

67. Dr. William R. Hunt delivered Elvis at the Presley's home on Old Saltillo Road on 8 January 1935.

68. Elvis made his first professional stage appearance on 30 July 1954 at Overton Park in Memphis.

69. Elvis loves pillow fights with teenage girls.

70. Elvis married Priscilla in Las Vegas on 1 May 1967.

71. Elvis never carries his own money. Even when he was quite young he always asked someone else to carry his wallet.

72. Elvis has never been known to smoke. According to one friend, "the Colonel introduced him to cigars, but while the Colonel smoked them, Elvis ate them. He chewed them till there was nothing left but the stub." His favourite brand is Hav-a-Tampa.

73. Elvis did not ever think of his performances as being scandalous. "Man, I was tame compared to what they do now," he said in 1972. "I didn't do anything but jiggle."

74. Elvis often consults with astrologers.

75. Elvis often uses the pseudonym Colonel Jon Burrows.

76. Elvis on karate: "It's an art, not a sport. It involved the Buddhist monks. They had no way of protecting themselves from robbers. So they studied the different animals. They studied the tiger..."

77. Elvis once gave Sammy Davis jun. a 157-carat black sapphire ring.

78. According to rating figures, 40 million viewers watched the *Milton Berle Show*, in which Elvis starred on 3 April 1956. A spokesman for the show boasted: "That's one out of every four folks in the US tuned in to us."

79. An inventory of Elvis' effects after his "death" said he had "20 pairs of pyjamas with matching hats" that hung near his bedside.

80. An old Elvis guitar fetched a record price of $33,000 at a recent auction.

81. As a young boy, Elvis' favourite comic book hero was *Captain Marvel*.

82. At a press conference just after leaving the army, Elvis said his favourite record was *Now or Never* and his best job of acting *King Creole*.

83. Elvis once had a Cadillac covered with 40 coats of paint containing crushed diamonds and oriental fish scales. The ceiling was covered with gold records - and the inside with gold plated gadgets.

84. Elvis once told his half-brother, Billy Stanley, that he was one-quarter Cherokee.

85. Elvis orders bacon instead of hamburger meat in his cheeseburgers.

86. Elvis owned 37 guns and rifles when he "died", including a sawn-off shotgun, according to an official inventory of his effects.

87. Elvis performed at a concert in Kalamazoo on 26 April 1977. He has been seen there several times since his "death".

88. The King planned to marry Ginger Alden on Christmas Day 1977.

89. Elvis played the piano at a concert for the first time on 19 July 1975, at Uniondale, New York.

90. Elvis prefers Prell Shampoo for Dyed Hair and a hairspray called Presto.

91. The King used a blond wig as a disguise to fool fans, according to a 1976 news report

92. Elvis proposed to Memphis beauty Ginger Alden (born 1954) on 26 January 1977 because *Cheiro's Book of Numbers* showed that would be the ideal date.

93. Elvis rarely takes a bath or a shower.

94. "Who are they?" asked Elvis when told that the Rolling Stones, already a famous rock group, wanted to meet him.

95. When it comes to boots, Elvis prefers black, white or blue patent leather Verdis or San Remos.

96. Elvis reads his horoscope every day.

97. The King received a threatening letter in 1964 which said the Red Army was planning to assassinate him.

98. Elvis received his first guitar, which cost $12.95, in January 1946 from his father, Vernon, who had ordered it by mail.

A 15-year-old schoolgirl revealed that she turns off the light in her room before she undresses to go to bed. The Reason: 'I have 1003 photographs of Elvis stuck on my bedroom walls — all smiling down at me. It makes me feel shy.'

— London newspaper report, 1957

99. Elvis recorded 136 gold and 10 platinum records - more than any other artist.

100. Elvis refuses to wear jeans in real life because, he told friends, he does not want to be reminded of his poverty-stricken childhood.

101. Elvis served as a jeep driver in the army.

102. Elvis received his Tennessee driver's licence, number 2571459, on 18 September 1975.

103. The King signed his first recording contract, for three years with Sun Records, on 19 July 1954.

104. Elvis' favourite sport at Graceland was called *War* and was played with firecrackers.

105. Elvis started dating at the age of 15. He first went steady with Betty McMann, then Billie Wardlow, followed by Dixie Locke, whom he met in February 1954.

106. The King recorded *Blue Suede Shoes*, written by Carl Perkins, on 31 January 1956.

107. Elvis started to stutter while in Junior High School in Memphis because "the kids were inviting me to parties so they could make fun of me."

108. Elvis wore a Star of David around his neck for several years before his "death". He told friends: "I wouldn't want to be kept out of heaven on a technicality."

109. The King stayed up all night before reporting for army service - because he hates to get up early in the morning. "Those guys (in the army) get up about the time I go to bed," he said.

110. Elvis pillow talk: feet are "sooties" (from "footies").

111. The King took his musical theme from Strauss' *Also Sprach Zarathustra*, the theme from the movie *2001*.

112. Elvis used karate in several of his movies.

113. The King used the royalties from *Heartbreak Hotel* to buy Graceland for $100,000.

114. Elvis wanted to be a famous football star - but was thrown out of the high school team because he refused to have a haircut.

115. Elvis was 32 when he married Priscilla.

116. The King "died" aged 42 years, seven months, and eight days, on 16 August 1977.

117. Elvis was a huge hit in Las Vegas on 27 February 1969 when he made his first appearance in eight years.

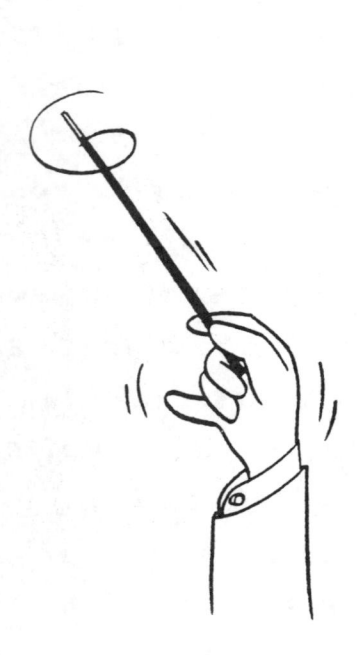

118. Religion was always important to Elvis and, according to his half-brother, Billy Stanley, he often held his own Bible meetings at Graceland and at his house in Bel Air. "He'd gather a group, read passages from the Old or New Testament, and then ask everyone their interpretations of what he'd read," Billy wrote later. "However, sometimes Elvis would get so excited that he couldn't wait for the interpretations of others. He'd cut them off and tell his own."

119. Elvis was appointed an honorary Tennessee Colonel on 8 March 1961.

120. The King was arrested for speeding on 7 July 1958 while he was driving back to his army base from home.

121. Elvis was born at 4.35 a.m. on 8 January 1935, at Tupelo, Mississippi.

122. In 1977, British actress Diana Dors disclosed a five-month love affair with Elvis during which, she claimed, they spoke of marriage. She said her "wild, wild love affair" in the mid-1950s was one of the best-kept secrets of show-business. "I loved him with all my heart," she proclaimed. They met when Diana was 24 and Elvis was 21.

123. Elvis is fascinated by Rudolf Valentino's hold over women.

124. Elvis was first threatened with arrest for an "obscene" performance on 11 August 1956 in Florida. The fans, naturally, loved the show.

125. In 1978 the Statler Hilton Hotel in New York City held an exhibition of four life-size Elvis dummies, draped in traditional, sequined Elvis finery. The dummies were so authentic they even perspired. Fans paid $5 to $10 per person and the show made a fortune.

126. Elvis as a youth was not a great reader - which was one reason why he became a rock star. Explained the King: "Maybe I took to playing a guitar and singing because I wasn't much good with books in high school ... Because I was more noticed among the girls, I felt more important."

127. Elvis was not yet 19 when he landed his first full-time job: driving a truck for Crown Electric.

128. Women's feet fascinate the King. "The minute I see a woman's feet," he often said, "I know if I like her or not."

129. Elvis was only 22 when he first bought Graceland. He paid $100,000 for the 18-room mansion.

130. Elvis was originally "buried" at the Forest Hills Cemetery, Midtown, Memphis, on 18 August 1977. The coffin was later transferred to Meditation Gardens at Graceland.

131. On 5 March 1960 Sergeant Elvis Presley was released from the US Army.

132. The King cut *Heartbreak Hotel* at the RCA studio in Nashville on 10

> "At the moment you have a million dollars worth of talent, but after I'm through with you, you'll have a million dollars."
> - Col Tom Parker to Elvis on signing a contract to manage him.

January 1956.

133. Elvis was so impressed with General Douglas MacArthur's "Old Soldiers Never Die" farewell speech that he memorised it at high school.

134. Walking tall has always been an Elvis habit: he wears shoes with an inch-and-a-half (3.8cm) heel.

135. Elvis' act at first was known as *The Hillbilly Cat*.

136. The King's co-star in his first movie, *Love Me Tender*, was Debra Paget.

137. Elvis' coffin was carried in a white Cadillac hearse, licence number 1-CF653.

138. Elvis' eighteenth birthday gift from his father was a 1942 Lincoln Zephyr coupe, his first car, which cost $50.

139. The King's eyes are blue/hazel.

140. Vernon Presley was a skilled carpenter and house painter, who also worked as a truck driver.

141. Elvis' favourite dish from the Deep South is corn pone.

142. Elvis' fiancee Ginger Alden claimed in May 1978 that she was in communication with Elvis - in psychic dreams.

143. The King's first album after being released from the army was called *Elvis Is Back!*

144. At Graceland today there is a five-foot replica of the wedding cake Elvis and Priscilla cut on 1 May 1967.

145. Elvis recorded *Hound Dog* on 2 July 1956.

146. At Graceland, Elvis loved putting on scuba-diving gear, then sitting at the bottom of the pool watching pretty girls in skimpy bikinis swim around him.

147. As a high school student, Elvis dreamed of the day he could be a Tennessee State Highway Patrolman.

148. Elvis' first newspaper interview took place on 28 July 1954 with Edwin Howard of the Memphis *Press-Scimitar*.

149. At the start of his stage career, Elvis' favourite outfits included a bright red or green sports jacket, navy trousers, red socks, and white shoes with blue soles.

150. Elvis' "funeral" cost $46,464. In addition, there was a bill of $6000 from the Memphis police for security.

151. Elvis' hair is naturally light-brown.

152. The King's karate name is Tiger.

153. Gladys Presley originally misspelt Elvis' middle name, Aaron, as Aron. He had his name legally changed in 1963.

154. Elvis' mother and father were married on 17 June 1933.

155. The King's nickname for himself in the sixties was *Crazy*. He even had it inscribed on a bracelet which he wore.

156. Elvis' parents appeared very briefly in *Loving You*, his second movie, where they feature in a crowd scene.

157. Elvis' personal staff was known as the Memphis Mafia.

158. The Elvis TV show *Aloha from Hawaii* was simulcast via satellite to 40 countries on 14 January 1973.

159. Jesse Garon Presley, Elvis' twin brother, was stillborn at 4 a.m. on 8 January 1935 - 35 minutes before the King.

160. Elvis' favourite board game is Monopoly. He spent the evening of his 40th birthday challenging all-comers to a game, according to friends.

161. Elvis, at home, would go into his bedroom and change his clothes every 15 minutes, according to an old friend, P.J. Proby.

162. Interviewed on the set of *Love Me Tender*, Elvis admitted his ambition to star in a movie about the life of James Dean: "I could do it easy. I want to play that more than anything else."

163. Elvis, who made it to the top singing about a special hound dog, lavished a small fortune in medical care on his pet male chow named Getlow, in 1975. The dog, at the age of 10 months, spent nearly two months in a veterinary hospital where it was treated for near-fatal kidney failure. When discharged, the dog flew from Massachusetts to Tennessee as the lone passenger in Presley's personal Lear jet.

164. Fifteen Elvis supporters were jailed for between six months and four-and-a-half years for staging a pro-Presley march in Leipzig in November 1959.

165. Gangsters swindled Elvis out of his Jetstar plane, according to his FBI file.

166. Elvis prefers a Wilkinson straight razor; he sometimes also uses an electric razor.

167. Girlfriend Linda Thompson presented Elvis with a plaque for the side of his bed on which was inscribed his favourite biblical verses from Corinthians I, Chapter 13.

168. Gladys Presley kept chickens even when she lived at Graceland.

169. Elvis' coffin was covered with 500 red rose-buds.

170. Graceland was built in 1939.

171. *Heartbreak Hotel* was the first record ever to hit No. 1 simultaneously on the pop and country charts.

172. Elvis served in the US 3rd Armoured (Spearhead) Division in

"It's not what he sings, but the way he sings it. His numbers are hilly-billy, but his manner can only be described, without lapsing into bad taste, as Rock 'n' Roll. For it describes, in its writhing, squirming aggression, one thing, sex. See him at work and you know why youngsters squeal and elders protest. And why he is called 'The Pelvis.'"

- US review of *Love Me Tender*, 1956.

STAY AWAY FROM ELVIS! Students at Notre Dame Convent have been asked to stay away from the visiting US singer and sign the following declaration: "I promise that I shall not take part in the reception accorded Elvis Presley and I shall not be present at the programme presented by him at the Auditorium, Wednesday', April 3, 1957. Signed ..." (Eight girls defied this ruling and were later expelled from the convent.)
- Canadian newspaper report.

Germany from 1958 to 1960.

173. Herbert von Karajan, conductor of the Berlin Philharmonic Orchestra, offered this explanation in 1956 of Elvis and rock music: "Strange things happen in the bloodstream when a musical resonance coincides with the beat of the human pulse."

174. If Elvis and Priscilla had a boy, they planned to name him John Baron.

175. Elvis was introduced in pubs as "the poor man's Liberace" In 1953.

176. In 1957, the Mexican Government banned Elvis because he "lacks aesthetic values and is markedly pornographic". The ban was announced by Education Minister Jose Angel Ceniceros. He said Elvis would not be permitted to perform in government-owned theatres.

177. Elvis has sold over one billion records - and the number is still rising.

178. In 1958, Elvis owned four Cadillacs: one pink-and-black, another canary yellow, one white and one plain black

179. Elvis recorded *Teddy Bear* on 23 February 1957.

180. In high school, Elvis belonged to the army cadets, the Biology Club, English Club, History Club and Speech Club.

181. *Kissin' Cousins*, released on 6 March 1964, featured Elvis wearing a blond wig.

182. Graceland's original address, Highway 51 South, Memphis, Tennessee, was changed to 3764 Elvis Presley Boulevard to honour its famous resident.

183. In *Love Me Tender* Elvis played the role of Clint Reno.

184. Elvis' favourite horse at his Circle G Ranch was a Palomino called Rising Sun. Priscilla's horse was named Domino.

185. Elvis' favourite karate reading includes magazines such as *Black Belt, Inside Kung Fu*, and *Fighting Stars*.

186. Intensive touring and his dedication to his art took its toll of Elvis. By September 1957 he confessed: "I lose myself in my singing. Maybe it's my early training singing gospel hymns. I'm limp as a rag, worn out when a show's over. I had a couple of nervous breakdowns a while back when I was making too many of these one night stands."

187. Elvis' first concert appearance was at the Overton Park Shell in Memphis on 30 July 1954. He was not the star, but performed as part of the bill for Slim Whitman.

188. At carnivals, Elvis loves throwing a baseball at wooden bottles.

189. It has been reported that Lloyds of London gave Elvis a clean bill of health for insurance purposes shortly before his "death".

190. *It's Now Or Never* had to wait six months for release in Britain -

because of copyright problems with the Italian melody.

191. *Jailhouse Rock* was banned in many towns throughout Britain after being slammed as "sex-crazed and disgusting" by British film critics. London critics described the film as "an unsavoury, nauseating and muddy brew of delinquency, bad taste and violence". In Australia, church leaders and psychiatrists also called for the film to be banned.

192. In Tupelo, Elvis' birthplace, the Mayor declared 16 August an official day of mourning "for all time".

193. Jerry Lee Lewis once turned up at Graceland in the early hours of the morning waving a pistol and daring Elvis to come out.

194. In an interview with a British newspaper in September 1959, Elvis' father said: "I don't foresee marriage for Elvis in the immediate future. When he's asked what type of girl he prefers, he just says 'female'."

195. John Lennon wore a false beard and dark glasses to avoid fans when he visited Elvis alone at Graceland.

196. Elvis' first law-enforcement job, which he landed on 21 September 1964, was as special deputy to the sheriff of Shelby County.

197. Larry Geller became Elvis' personal hair stylist in April 1964.

198. Elvis' first contract with Sun Records was sold to RCA for less than $48,000.

199. Lisa Marie's middle name was chosen by Elvis and Priscilla in honour of Colonel Tom Parker's wife.

200. *Love Me Tender* was Elvis' first movie.

201. Gladys Love Smith (Elvis' mother) was born on 25 April 1912 in Pototuc County, Mississippi, one of 10 children.

202. Lisa Marie owns Graceland, which is being held in trust for her until she turns 25 in 1993.

203. Elvis' father, Vernon, died of heart failure at 9.20 a.m. on 26 June 1979. He was 63.

204. *Love Me Tender*, the title song from Elvis' first film, was the first record to have advance orders of more than one million in the USA.

205. Mary Tyler Moore was Elvis' leading lady in his last movie, *Change Of Habit*.

206. In *Loving You* Elvis played a Southern country singer named Deke Rivers.

207. A Miss Robbie Moore was awarded $5500 in an out-of-court settlement with Elvis, newspapers reported in September 1956. Miss Moore, then a 20-year-old Memphis telephone operator, had accused Elvis of invading her privacy, and of assault and battery. The assault? Elvis

"Someone has wisely said, 'The 1950s will be remarkable in history for their worship of mediocrity'. Let us hope the much ballyhooed Mr. P flouts this analysis."
- British *Record Mirror*, 1956.

had seized the sandwich she was eating in a cafe and ate most of it. The invasion of privacy? Uninvited, Elvis had laid his head on her shoulder. She sued when the photo of the incident was published in a fan magazine.

208. No Elvis movie ever lost money.

209. Lisa Marie Presley was born at 5.01 a.m. on 1 February 1968.

210. On 30 May 1977, a psychic named Gloria James predicted on a radio station in Boston that Elvis would die "soon".

211. Graceland is visited by 2500 Elvis fans a day.

212. When on a health food diet, Elvis eats huge quantities of yoghurt and ripe honeydew melon.

213. *Love Me Tender*, the hit from Elvis' first film, is based on a Civil War song.

214. On Memphis station WHBQ, Dewey Phillips became the first disc jockey to play an Elvis Presley record on the radio. The date? 7 July 1954.

215. When he appeared on The Ed Sullivan Show, Elvis was shown only from the waist up.

216. On the memorial to his mother at Forest Hills Cemetery, Elvis had inscribed: "She Was The Sunshine Of Our Home".

217. One of Elvis' favourite haunts while in the army in Germany was the Moulin Rouge in Munich.

218. It has been claimed that Priscilla dyed her hair black at Elvis' request because he'd been captivated by the way Debra Paget's hair looked in his first movie, *Love Me Tender*.

219. Gladys Presley (Elvis' mother) died in hospital on 14 August 1958.

220. Priscilla's pet name for Elvis is "fire eyes".

221. Quote from a Sydney newspaper in late 1956: "Perhaps the best news for parents is that the rock 'n roll craze already seems to be dying out overseas. This debased and over-simplified form of music, designed specifically for the hit parades, seems destined to go the way of most hit-parade music - to oblivion."

222. Gladys Presley once said that, unlike some children, Elvis never needed any prodding to go to church.

223. Quote from East Germany's youth newspaper in 1958, while Elvis was in the army: "The 23-year-old star Presley is no artist and enjoys only limited brain power." It added that "people who believe in atomic war as the final solution for all political problems" were parading Elvis as a prominent personality.

224. Priscilla once surprised Elvis by installing 3 spray nozzles in his shower so his entire body could be sprayed simultaneously.

Please turn to Page 81

The Exclusive Priscilla Presley Mask!

Elvis fell in love with Priscilla when she was still a schoolgirl and, say friends, he has never stopped loving her. So one of the best ways to attract the King's attention - and persuade him to reveal himself - would be to look like Priscilla looked when they first fell in love. That's the purpose of this exclusive mask - to help you snare Elvis through love!

Assembling the mask is simple - just follow the instructions below, preferably while humming LOVE ME TENDER.

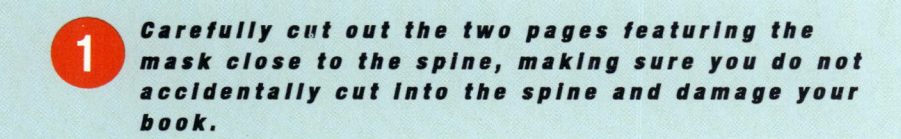

1 Carefully cut out the two pages featuring the mask close to the spine, making sure you do not accidentally cut into the spine and damage your book.

2 For added strength, glue both sections onto a piece of flexible cardboard, making sure the overlapping sections of the hair line up. While doing this, hum TEDDY BEAR to get you into the right frame of mind.

3 Cut out the mask carefully around the edges of the face and hair. Cut out eyeholes to suit. Make two holes on the earrings and affix elastic or string. NOTE: If you don't want to punch holes through the earlobes, you can staple the string or elastic to the cardboard.

4 Wear a sexy dress or else hide your body behind a pot plant so that only the mask is visible. The beehive is tall enough to act as an Elvis antenna should he be anywhere within your line of vision. Standing on a high hill or skyscraper while wearing the mask would give you a lead on the other Elvis Spotters.
PS: When speaking to the King, remember NO SWEARING and put your best foot forward (he loved women's feet).

PRISCILLA MASK!

Fun For The Whole Family!

Love Me Tender

When Elvis first saw schoolgirl Priscilla Beaulieu while serving in the Army in Germany in 1959, he exclaimed: "She looks like an angel!" He thought she had "a cute face" - but decided her hair needed some alterations before she fitted his idea of perfection.

So the King persuaded Priscilla to dye her hair deep black (so she resembled Debra Paget in the movie *Love Me Tender*) and wear it in a high beehive style.

The hairdo was so huge that a Memphis Mafia member once remarked: "She looked like she had about eight people living in her hair."

Elvis fondly called her "Cilla"; she nicknamed him "Fire Eyes". They were married in Las Vegas on 1 May 1967 by Judge David Zenoff.

Sadly, they separated on 23 February 1972 and divorced the following year, but even then Elvis still loved her so much he refused to collect his final copy of the divorce papers.

225. RCA-Victor presented Elvis with a diamond-studded wrist watch in January 1961. The back of the watch was engraved with the King's combined sales figures for the previous five years - 76 million records.

226. Priscilla Presley attained a green belt in karate.

227. Quote from Elvis' cousin Hershell Presley on the young King: "I remember Elvis used to carry that guitar around. He loved that guitar. It didn't have but three strings on it most of the time, but he sure could beat the dickens outta it."

228. "READING POLITICS. Elvis Presley, who used to describe karate as his main hobby, has recently been reading extensively, and is particularly interested in politics ..." - News report, August 1961.

229. Lisa Marie weighed 6 pounds, 15 ounces at birth.

230. Roman Catholics who had succumbed to Elvis Presley should pray for themselves, said the official Catholic organ in Australia, *Southern Cross*, in June 1958. "They should pray for the wisdom to seek the better gifts and not to saturate themselves with the second best... Presley 'sends' many young Catholics, yet they know he is a kind of patron saint of larrikin groups." The paper also recommended prayers for Presley "that he may be a good, humble reverent man and save his soul".

231. Elvis' first record, *That's Alright, Mama*, sold 7000 copies within a week.

232. Schoolboy Elvis' singing heroes were Dean Martin and Frankie Laine.

233. The call-sign for Elvis' Convair 880 plane was Eight-eighty Echo Papa.

234. Priscilla was not mentioned in Elvis' will.

235. Quote from Elvis before sailing for Germany with the army: "The first place I want to go to is Paris to visit Brigitte Bardot."

236. The *Elvis - Aloha from Hawaii* concert was watched by an estimated 1.5 billion people worldwide.

237. The famous music gate was installed at Graceland in April 1957.

238. The FBI kept a 633-page file on Elvis for more than 20 years.

239. The first Elvis record to be broadcast on radio was *That's Alright Mama* on station WHB2, on 7 March 1954.

240. The flip side of Elvis' first record, *That's Alright, Mama*, was *Blue Moon of Kentucky*.

241. When Elvis and Priscilla married, the ceremony was performed by Judge David Zenoff.

242. The first movie featuring Elvis with dyed hair was *Loving You*.

> *Even Jesus wasn't loved in his day.*
> — Elvis to his critics in the fifties who considered him too sexy.

> "I'm The Killer, but Elvis will always be The King."
> — Jerry Lee Lewis

> "The Beatles wouldn't have happened had he not been around."
> — Paul McCartney about Elvis.

243. When Elvis performed at his high school's annual variety show, he received the most applause - and was rewarded with a chance to perform the show's only encore.

244. The report of the County Medical Examiner in Memphis states that Elvis' "corpse" weighed 170 pounds - a great deal less than the 200 to 250 pounds he was estimated to have weighed by people who saw him in his last weeks.

245. The TV series *Kung Fu*, starring David Carradine, is one of Elvis' favourites.

246. The University of Tennessee at Knoxville offers a course entitled: *The Cultural Phenomenon of Elvis Presley: The Making of a Folk Hero.*

247. Elvis' father, Vernon, divorced his second wife, Dee, in November 1977.

248. Two weeks after Elvis' "death" three men were arrested at midnight attempting to break into his mausoleum in Forest Hills Cemetery, Memphis, to steal his body. Police said a $10 million ransom demand was planned.

249. When Elvis was about 10, he took to firing his airgun at elderly women at a bus stop. "They had their rears facing us and the pellets stunned them," recalls Elvis' childhood friend, Billy Smith. "Elvis was rolling on the floor laughing. But he didn't do it anymore after his father, Vernon, caught him and spanked him. He was always up to mischief."

250. Vernon Presley remarried on 3 June 1960 and became step-father to Davada (Dee) Stanley's three sons, David, Rick and Billy.

251. The first take at Elvis' first professional recording session with Sun Records was *I love You Because*.

252. Until his "death", Elvis earned around $4.3 billion.

253. The flip side of the Elvis record breaker *Hound Dog* was another hit: *Don't Be Cruel*.

254. What did the Colonel know? Colonel Tom Parker came to Elvis' funeral dressed in a Hawaiian shirt and baseball cap and studiously avoided looking at the coffin.

255. When Elvis appeared at Las Vegas, so many women threw their underwear at him that the ladies' room started to stock panties and other underwear.

256. What is the secret of Elvis' success? Said the King: "I came along when there was no trend in music and people were looking for one."

257. When Elvis gave a press conference after his arrival in Germany while in the army, he was asked: "Do you like classical music?" Elvis replied: "It puts me to sleep. I mean, it doesn't say anything to me."

258. Elvis' first recording session with RCA was held on 11 January 1956 - three days after his 21st birthday.

259. What's the origin of *Hound Dog*? Jerry Leibner, who co-wrote the hit with Mike Stoller, confessed in 1959: "Mike did this spontaneous roll-out, and there was something nasty in the music. I just blurted out: 'You ain't nuthin' but a hound dog!' and there it was."

260. Vernon Presley, Elvis' father, was born on 19 April 1916 in Hulton, Mississippi.

261. When Elvis made his first appearance on TV on 13 July 1956, leading US critics dismissed him as a "joke".

262. "It's worse than my first night on television!" said Elvis on his arrival at Fort Hood, Texas, to start his eight weeks basic training in the army in March 1958.

263. "This cat came out in red pants and a green coat and a pink shirt and socks, and he had this sneer on his face and he stood behind the mike for five minutes, I'll bet, before he made a move. Then he hit his guitar a few licks, and he broke two strings. So there he was, these two strings dangling, and he hadn't done anything yet, and these high school girls were screaming and fainting and running up to the stage, and then he started to move his hips real slow like he had a thing for his guitar." - Country singer Bob Luman describing an early Elvis concert.

264. When Elvis performed to a capacity crowd at the Memorial Stadium in Spokane in August 1957, the organisers had only one complaint about the behaviour of the fans: they stole soil from the stadium in-field where the King's feet had touched it.

265. Elvis recorded *Baby, Let's Play House* early in his career and inserted a reference to his favourite car: a pink Cadillac.

266. "A 15-year-old schoolgirl revealed that she turns off the light in her room before she undresses to go to bed," reported a London newspaper in 1957. The reason: "I have 1003 photographs of Elvis stuck on my bedroom walls - all smiling down at me. It makes me feel shy."

267. Elvis' one and only performance at The Grand Ole Opry, temple of country music, was on 25 September 1954.

268. When Elvis tried out for the chorus at high school, he was told he did not have the "right kind of voice".

269. Elvis' nickname for Priscilla was "Cilla".

270. When Elvis turned 40, it was revealed he liked 12 hours sleep every night.

The Chief of Police will not permit Elvis Presley to perform any "lewd, lascivious contortions that would excite a crowd" when the rock 'n' roll singer appears at Louisville on November 25.

- News report from Kentucky November 1956

271. The King's number in the army was US53310761.

272. "Elvis was really a prude. Girls lost their appeal for him when they were easy to get. He always said that he wanted to marry a virgin." - Sonny West, a friend since high school, about the young Elvis.

273. When Elvis was 15 he worked at a movie theatre from 5 p.m. to 10 p.m. for $12.50 a week.

274. Elvis and Priscilla legally separated on 23 February 1972.

275. When Elvis was growing up, he once told Billy Stanley, "We had two rooms, both smaller than any in this house (Graceland), bare floor, no heat 'cept when we were cooking, and no running water. And those were the good times! When we came to Memphis it got worse."

276. "Goodbye, darling, we loved you!" That's how a weeping Elvis' farewelled his mother at her funeral in August 1958.

277. Elvis and Priscilla were divorced on 9 October 1973, yet amazingly Elvis never collected his final copy of the divorce papers.

278. "What do you think of teenagers?" Elvis was asked at a New York press conference in 1956. "Ah'd be lost without them," he replied. What did he think of the Texas fans who almost pulled his Cadillac to bits? "Ah can't grumble," came the laconic answer. "They bought it."

279. Elvis always has at hand a large religious and mystical library. Favourites include The Bible, *The Prophet*, *The Impersonal Life*, *Autobiography of a Yoga*, *The Initiation of the World*, *Beyond the Himalayas*, *The Secret Doctrine*, *The Urantia Book*, *The Fourth Way*, *The Mystical Christ*, *Leaves of Morya's Garden*, *Adventure in Consciousness*, and *Cheiro's Book of Numbers*.

280. Elvis always insisted to his friends that he would communicate with them after death.

281. "When I went on, I heard people screaming, but it all happened so fast. I just went with it. All I knew was, the only way to do it, the only way to make it, what got me to this point, was just to be natural and let it happen. And don't stop. Don't stop anything. Don't think. The minute I started thinking, it would turn off. So, you don't think. Just do it. Just be it." - Elvis about his first appearance on the Ed Sullivan Show.

282. The King recorded *Are You Lonesome Tonight* on 4 April 1960

283. When Madame Tussaud's in London first put up a model of Elvis in 1978, it moved many fans to tears – of anger. Newspaper reports said most fans thought it bore a closer resemblance to TV's *Incredible Hulk* than to their idol.

284. Elvis believes his mother's ghost haunts Graceland. Friends said he

---

"I've usually been very nervous when I go on stage, but I'd always stop shaking once I start singing. Sometimes I'd forget one of the lyrics of a song when I was in the middle of my act, but no one ever knew. I guess they couldn't tell what I was singing anyway!"

- Elvis

claimed to have spoken to her since her death in the house in 1958. Priscilla once said: "He often says he can still feel her around him."

285. When Elvis was in the army, he had his father write home to Memphis to order five boxes of a vitamin food, which he had been taking before being enlisted. According to Memphis nurseryman J.F. Ashworth who filled the order, the food contained alfalfa, watercress and parsley. Ashworth added: "I don't think Elvis has tired blood."

286. Elvis' blue-and-white Convair 880 jet, named for Lisa Marie, had a queen-size bed, four TV sets and a conference room.

287. Elvis brushes his teeth with Colgate.

288. When Elvis was in the army, it cost the services of six men around the clock to protect him from rock fans.

289. Elvis called his hairdresser, Larry Geller, his "guru" and bought him a new white Cadillac convertible.

290. When the King and Queen of Nepal visited Hollywood, they had only one request: to see Elvis, then filming *G.I. Blues*. They not only did, but came away with a new royal treasure: his autograph.

291. With his very first royalty cheque, Elvis bought his mother a pink Cadillac.

292. Elvis can swallow half-a-dozen and more tablets at once - and will demonstrate this ability with pride.

293. When Elvis was three, his father, Vernon, served on a prison chain-gang for forgery.

294. Elvis choreographed the title number of *Jailhouse Rock*.

295. When Elvis went to the movies, he avoided fans by hiring the entire cinema from midnight for himself and close friends.

296. Elvis cannot stand women who swear.

297. The King deodorises himself with Brut.

298. Elvis did his first screen test on April Fool's Day 1956.

299. When Elvis writhed and sang before a capacity crowd of 11,000 spectators in St Louis' Kiel Auditorium, he was shimmering in sequins and a metallic gold cloth suit which promoter Lee Gordon said had cost $2500. "It's real gold," crowed Gordon, "with impregnated unborn calf skin, or something of the sort."

300. Elvis disliked the term Memphis Mafia for his associates. He preferred the acronym *TCB* (Taking Care of Business) and personally designed the logo, which featured the letters TCB with a gold thunderbolt crashing through them.

KING HITS

★ Between 1954 and his "death" in 1977, Elvis Presley released 105 singles, 32 extended play albums and 65 LPs. To know the King you MUST know his work - so here is a complete chronological listing of his releases.

Sun 45-rpm and 78-rpm singles

1. **Sun 209** (August 1954) *That's All Right (Mama)/Blue Moon of Kentucky*
2. **Sun 210** (October 1954) *Good Rockin' Tonight/I Don't Care if the Sun Don't Shine*
3. **Sun 215** (January 1955) *Milkcow Blues Boogie/You're a Heartbreaker*
4. **Sun 217** (May 1955) *I'm Left, You're Right, She's Gone/Baby, Let's Play House*
5. **Sun 223** (August 1955) *Mystery Train/I Forgot to Remember to Forget*

RCA 45-rpm and 78-rpm singles

1. **RCA 6357** (November 1955) *Mystery Train/I Forgot to Remember to Forget*
2. **RCA 6380** (November 1955) *That's All Right (Mama)/Blue Moon of Kentucky*
3. **RCA 6381** (November 1955) *Good Rockin' Tonight/I Don't Care if the Sun Don't Shine*
4. **RCA 6382** (November 1955) *Milkcow Blues Boogie/You're a Heartbreaker*
5. **RCA 6383** (November 1955) *I'm Left, You're Right, She's Gone/Baby, Let's Play House*
6. **RCA 6420** (January 1956) *Heartbreak Hotel/I Was the One*
7. **RCA 6540** (May 1956) *I Want You, I Need You, I Love You/My Baby Left Me*
8. **RCA 6604** (July 1956) *Hound Dog/Don't Be Cruel*
9. **RCA 6636** (September 1956) *Blue Suede Shoes/Tutti Frutti*
10. **RCA 6637** (September 1956) *I'm Counting on You/I Got a Woman*
11. **RCA 6638** (September 1956) *I'll Never Let You Go/I'm Gonna Sit Right Down and Cry over You*
12. **RCA 6639** (September 1956) *Tryin' to Get to You/I Love You Because*
13. **RCA 6640** (September 1956) *Blue Moon/Just Because*
14. **RCA 6641** (September 1956) *Money Honey/One-sided Love Affair*
15. **RCA 6642** (September 1956) *Shake, Rattle and Roll/Lawdy, Miss Clawdy*
16. **RCA 6643** (September 1956) *Love Me Tender/Any Way You Want Me*
17. **RCA 6800** (January 1957) *Too Much/Playing for Keeps*
18. **RCA 6870** (March 1957) *All Shook Up/That's When Your Heartaches Begin*
19. **RCA 7000** (June 1957) *Teddy Bear/Loving You*
20. **RCA 7035** (September 1957) *Jailhouse Rock/Treat Me Nice*
21. **RCA 7150** (December 1957) *Don't/I Beg of You*
22. **RCA 7240** (April 1958) *Wear My Ring Around Your Neck/Doncha' Think It's Time*
23. **RCA 7280** (June 1958) *Hard-headed Woman/Don't Ask Me Why*
24. **RCA 7410** (October 1958) *I Got Stung/One Night*
25. **RCA 7506** (March 1959) *A Fool Such as I/I Need Your Love Tonight*
26. **RCA 7600** (June 1959) *A Big Hunk o' Love/My Wish Came True*
27. **RCA 7740** (March 1960) *Stuck on You/Fame and Fortune*

Thanks a million to everybody, everywhere! You've been wonderful.

Current Song Rage . . .

"HOUND DOG"
b/w
"DON'T BE CRUEL"
RCA Victor 20/47-6604

28. **RCA 7777** (July 1960) *It's Now or Never/A Mess of Blues*
29. **RCA 7810** (November 1960) *Are You Lonesome Tonight?/I Gotta Know*
30. **RCA 7850** (February 1961) *Surrender/Lonely Man*
31. **RCA 7880** (May 1961) *I Feel So Bad/Wild in the Country*
32. **RCA 7908** (August 1961) *Little Sister/His Latest Flame*
33. **RCA 7968** (November 1961) *Can't Help Falling in Love/Rock-a-Hula Baby*
34. **RCA 7992** (February 1962) *Good Luck Charm/Anything That's Part of You*
35. **RCA 8041** (July 1962) *She's Not You/Just Tell Her Jim Said Hello*
36. **RCA 8100** (October 1962) *Return to Sender/Where Do You Come From*
37. **RCA 8134** (January 1963) *One Broken Heart for Sale/They Remind Me Too Much of You*
38. **RCA 8188** (July 1963) *Devil in Disguise/Please Don't Drag That String Around*
39. **RCA 8243** (October 1963) *Bossa Nova Baby/Witchcraft*
40. **RCA 8307** (February 1964) *Kissin' Cousins/It Hurts Me*
41. **RCA 0639** (April 1964) *Kiss Me Quick/Suspicion*
42. **RCA 8360** (May 1964) *Viva Las Vegas/What'd I Say*
43. **RCA 8400** (July 1964) *Such a Night/Never Ending*
44. **RCA 8440** (September 1964) *Ain't That Loving You, Baby/Ask Me*
45. **RCA 0720** (November 1964) *Blue Christmas/Wooden Heart*
46. **RCA 8500** (March 1965) *Do the Clam/You'll Be Gone*
47. **RCA 0643** (April 1965) *Crying in the Chapel/I Believe in the Man in the Sky*
48. **RCA 8585** (May 1965) *(Such an) Easy Question/It Feels So Right*
49. **RCA 8657** (August 1965) *I'm Yours/(It's a) Long Lonely Highway*
50. **RCA 0650** (October 1965) *Puppet on a String/Wooden Heart*
51. **RCA 0647** (November 1965) *Blue Christmas/Santa Claus Is Back in Town*
52. **RCA 8740** (January 1966) *Tell Me Why/Blue River*
53. **RCA 0651** (February 1966) *Joshua Fit the Battle/Known Only to Him*
54. **RCA 0652** (February 1966) *Milky White Way/Swing Down, Sweet Chariot*
55. **RCA 8780** (March 1966) *Frankie and Johnny/Please Don't Stop Loving Me*
56. **RCA 8870** (June 1966) *Love Letters/Come What May*
57. **RCA 8941** (October 1966) *Spinout/All That I Am*
58. **RCA 8950** (November 1966) *If Every Day Was Like Christmas/How Would You Like to Be*
59. **RCA 9056** (January 1967) *Indescribably Blue/Fools Fall in Love*
60. **RCA 9115** (May 1967) *Long-legged Girl/That's Someone You Never Forget*
61. **RCA 9287** (August 1967) *There's Always Me/Judy*
62. **RCA 9341** (September 1967) *Big Boss Man/You Don't Know Me*
63. **RCA 9425** (January 1968) *Guitar Man/High-heel Sneakers*
64. **RCA 9465** (March 1968) *U.S. Male/Stay Away*
65. **RCA 9600** (April 1968) *You'll Never Walk Alone/We Call on Him*
66. **RCA 9547** (May 1968) *Let Yourself Go/Your Time Hasn't Come Yet, Baby*
67. **RCA 9610** (September 1968) *A Little Less Conversation/Almost in Love*
68. **RCA 9670** (October 1968) *If I Can Dream/Edge of Reality*
69. **RCA 9731** (March 1969) *Memories/Charro!*
70. **RCA 0130** (April 1969) *How Great Thou Art/His Hand in Mine*
71. **RCA 9741** (April 1969) *In the Ghetto/Any Day Now*

"Perhaps the best news for parents is that the rock 'n roll craze already seems to be dying out overseas. This debased and over-simplified form of music, designed specifically for the hit parades, seems destined to go the way of most hit-parade music - to oblivion."

— Sydney newspaper report in late 1956.

72. **RCA 9747** (June 1969) *Clean Up Your Own Back Yard/The Fair Is Moving On*
73. **RCA 9764** (August 1969) *Suspicious Minds/You'll Think of Me*
74. **RCA 9768 -** (November 1969) *Don't Cry, Daddy/Rubberneckin'*
75. **RCA 9791** (January 1970) *Kentucky Rain/My Little Friend*
76. **RCA 9835** (May 1970) *The Wonder of You/Mama Liked the Roses*
77. **RCA 9873** (July 1970) *I've Lost You/The Next Step Is Love*
78. **RCA 9916** (October 1970) *You Don't Have to Say You Love Me/Patch It Up*
79. **RCA 9960** (December 1970) *I Really Don't Want to Know/There Goes My Everything*
80. **RCA 9980** (March 1971) *Rags to Riches/Where Did They Go, Lord*
81. **RCA 9985** (May 1971) *Life/Only Believe*
82. **RCA 9998** (August 1971) *I'm Leavin'/Heart of Rome*
83. **RCA 1017** (October 1971) *It's Only Love/The Sound of Your Cry*
84. RCA 0572 (November 1971) *Merry Christmas, Baby/O Come, All Ye Faithful*
85. **RCA 0619** (January 1972) *Until It's Time for You to Go/We Can Make the Morning*
86. **RCA 0651** (March 1972) *He Touched Me/The Bosom of Abraham*
87. **RCA 0672** (April 1972) *An American Trilogy/The First Time Ever I Saw Your Face*
88. **RCA 0769** (August 1972) *Burning Love/It's a Matter of Time*
89. **RCA 0815** (November 1972) *Always on My Mind/Separate Ways*
90. **RCA 0910** (March 1973) *Fool/Steamroller Blues*
91. **RCA 0088** (September 1973) *Raised on Rock/For Ol' Times Sake*
92. **RCA 0196** (January 1974) *Take Good Care of Her/I've Got a Thing About You, Baby*
93. **RCA 0280** (May 1974) *Help Me/If You Talk in Your Sleep*
94. **RCA 10074** (October 1974) *It's Midnight/Promised Land*
95. **RCA 10191** (January 1975) *My Boy/Thinking About You*
96. **RCA 10278** (April 1975) *T-R-O-U-B-L-E/Mr. Songman*
97. **RCA 10401** (October 1975) *Bringing It Back/Pieces of My Life*
98. **RCA 10601** (March 1976) *Hurt/For the Heart*
99. **RCA 10857** (December 1976) *Moody Blue/She Thinks I Still Care*
100. **RCA 10998** (June 1977) *Way Down/Pledging My Love*

RCA 45-rpm extended-plays

1. **RCA EPB-1254** (March 1956) *Elvis Presley* Side 1: *Blue Suede Shoes; I'm Counting on You*; Side 2: *I Got a Woman; One-sided Love Affair* Side 3: *Tutti Frutti; Tryin' to Get to You* Side 4: *I'm Gonna Sit Right Down and Cry; I'll Never Let You Go*

2. **RCA EPA-747** (March 1956) *Elvis Presley* Side 1: *Blue Suede Shoes; Tutti Frutti* Side 2: *I Got a Woman; Just Because*

3. **RCA EPA-821** (May 1956) *Heartbreak Hotel* Side 1: *Heartbreak Hotel; I Was the One* Side 2: *Money Honey; I Forgot to Remember to Forget*

4. **RCA EPA-830** (September 1956) *Shake, Rattle and Roll* Side 1: *Shake, Rattle and Roll; I Love You Because* Side 2: *Blue Moon; Laudy, Miss Claudy*

5. **RCA EPA-965** (October 1956) *Any Way You Want Me* Side 1: *Any Way You Want Me; I'm Left, You're Right, She's Gone* Side 2: *I Don't Care if the Sun Don't Shine; Mystery Train*

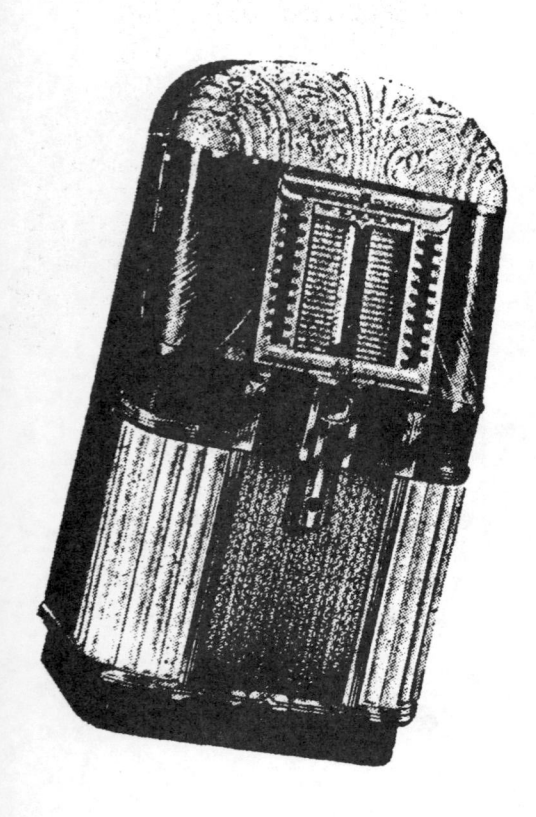

6. RCA EPA-940 (September 1956) *The Real Elvis* Side 1: *Don't Be Cruel; I Want You, I Need You, I Love You* Side 2: *Hound Dog; My Baby Left Me*

7. RCA EPA-5120 (First Gold Standard) (April 1961) *The Real Elvis* (features same songs as EPA-940).

8. RCA EPA-992 (November 1956) *Elvis, Volume I* Side 1: *Rip It Up; Love Me* Side 2: *When My Blue Moon Turns to Gold Again; Paralyzed*

9. RCA EPA-4006 (December 1956) *Love Me Tender* Side 1: *Love Me Tender; Let Me* Side 2: *Poor Boy; We're Gonna Move*

10. RCA EPA-993 (December 1956) *Elvis, Volume II* Side 1: *So Glad You're Mine; Old Shep* Side 2: *Ready Teddy; Anyplace Is Paradise*

11. RCA EPA-994 (January 1957) *Strictly Elvis* Side 1: *Long Tall Sally; First in Line* Side 2: *How Do You Think I Feel; How's the World Treating You*

12. RCA EPA-1-1515 (June 1957) *Loving You, Volume I* Side 1: *Loving You; Party* Side 2: *(Let Me Be Your) Teddy Bear; True Love*

13. RCA EPA-2-1515 (June 1957) *Loving You, Volume II* Side 1: *Lonesome Cowboy; Hot Dog* Side 2: *Mean Woman Blues; Got a Lot o' Livin' to Do!*

14. RCA EPA-4041 (September 1957) *Just for You* Side 1: *I Need You So; Have I Told You Lately That I Love You* Side 2: *Blueberry Hill; Is It So Strange*

15. RCA EPA-4054 (April 1957) *Peace in the Valley* Side 1: *(There'll Be) Peace in the Valley (for Me); It Is No Secret (What God Can Do)* Side 2: *I Believe; Take My Hand, Precious Lord*

16. RCA EPA-5121 (Gold Standard) (April 1961) *Peace in the Valley* (Features same songs as EPA-4054).

17. RCA EPA-4108 (November 1957) *Elvis Sings Christmas Songs* Side 1: *Santa, Bring My Baby Back (To Me); Blue Christmas* Side 2: *Santa Claus Is Back in Town; I'll Be Home for Christmas*

18. RCA EPA-4114 (November 1957) *Jailhouse Rock* Side 1: *Jailhouse Rock; Young and Beautiful* Side 2: *I Want to Be Free; Don't Leave Me Now; Baby, I Don't Care*

19. RCA EPA-4319 (October 1958) *King Creole, Volume I* Side 1: *King Creole; New Orleans* Side 2: *As Long As I Have You; Lover Doll*

20. RCA EPA-5122 (Gold Standard) (April 1961) *King Creole, Volume 1*

21. RCA EPA-4321 (October 1958) *King Creole, Volume II* Side 1: *Trouble; Young Dreams* Side 2: *Crawfish; Dixieland Rock*

22. RCA EPA-4325 (March 1959) *Elvis Sails* Side 1: *Media interviews with Elvis* Side 2: *More media interviews with Elvis*

23. RCA EPA-5157 (Gold Standard) (April 1961) *Elvis Sails*

24. RCA EPA-4340 (November 1958) *Christmas with Elvis* Side 1: *White Christmas; Here Comes Santa Claus* Side 2: *O Little Town of Bethlehem; Silent Night*

25. RCA EPA-5088 (Gold Standard) (April 1961) *A Touch of Gold, Volume I* Side 1: *Hard-headed Woman; Good Rockin' Tonight* Side 2: *Don't; I Beg of You*

26. RCA EPA-5101 (Gold Standard) (April 1961) *A Touch of Gold, Volume II* Side 1: *Wear My Ring Around Your Neck; Treat Me Nice* Side 2: *One Night; That's All Right*

27. RCA EPA-5141 (Gold Standard) (April 1961) *A Touch of Gold, Volume III* Side 1: *All Shook Up; Don't Ask Me Why* Side 2: *Too Much; Blue Moon of Kentucky*

28. RCA-4368 (May 1962) *Follow That Dream* Side 1: *Follow That Dream; Angel* Side 2: *What a Wonderful Life; I'm Not the Marrying Kind*

29. RCA EPA-4371 (September 1962) *Kid Galahad* Side 1: *King of the Whole*

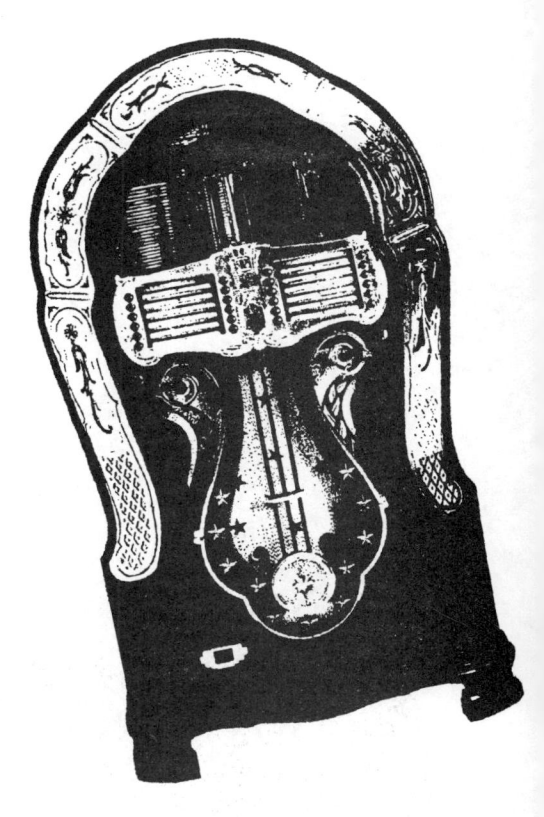

Wide World; This Is Living; Riding the Rainbow Side 2: Home Is Where the Heart Is; I Got Lucky; A Whistling Tune

30.   **RCA EPA-4382** (July 1964) *Viva Las Vegas* Side 1: *If You Think I Don't Need You; I Need Somebody to Lean On* Side 2: *C'mon, Everybody; Today, Tomorrow and Forever*

31.   **RCA EPA-4383** (July 1965) *Tickle Me* Side 1: *I Feel That I've Known You Forever; Slowly but Surely* Side 2: *Night Rider; Put the Blame on Me; Dirty, Dirty Feeling*

32.   **RCA EPA-4387** (May 1967) *Easy Come, Easy Go* Side 1: *Easy Come, Easy Go; The Love Machine; Yoga Is as Yoga Does* Side 2: *You Gotta Stop; Sing, You Children; I'll Take Love*

RCA long-playing albums

1.   **LPM-1254** (April 1956) *Elvis Presley* Side 1: *Blue Suede Shoes; I'm Counting on You; I Got a Woman; One-sided Love Affair; I Love You Because; Just Because* Side 2: *Tutti Frutti; Tryin' to Get to You; I'm Gonna Sit Right Down and Cry; I'll Never Let You Go; Blue Moon; Money Honey*

2.   **LPM-1382** (October 1956) *Elvis* Side 1: *Rip It Up; Love Me; When My Blue Moon Turns to Gold Again; Long Tall Sally; First in Line; Paralyzed* Side 2: *So Glad You're Mine; Old Shep; Ready Teddy; Anyplace Is Paradise; How's the World Treating You; How Do You Think I Feel*

3.   **LPM-1515** (July 1957) *Loving You* Side 1: *Mean Woman Blues; (Let Me Be Your) Teddy Bear; Loving You; Got a Lot o' Livin' to Do; Lonesome Cowboy; Hot Dog; Party* Side 2: *Blueberry Hill; True Love; Don't Leave Me Now; Have I Told You Lately That I Love You?; I Need You So*

4.   **LOC-1035** (November 1957) *Elvis' Christmas Album* Side 1: *Santa Claus Is Back in Town; White Christmas; Here Comes Santa Claus; I'll Be Home for Christmas; Blue Christmas; Santa, Bring My Baby Back (to Me).* Side 2: *O Little Town of Bethlehem; Silent Night; (There'll Be) Peace in the Valley (for Me); I Believe; Take My Hand, Precious Lord; It Is No Secret (What God Can Do)*

5.   **LPM-1707** (March 1958) *Elvis' Golden Records* Side 1: *Hound Dog; Loving You; All Shook Up; Heartbreak Hotel; Jailhouse Rock; Love Me; Too Much* Side 2: *Don't Be Cruel; That's When Your Heartaches Begin; Teddy Bear; Love Me Tender; Treat Me Nice; Any Way You Want Me; I Want You, I Need You, I Love You*

6.   **LPM-1884** (August 1958) *King Creole* Side 1: *King Creole; As Long As I Have You; Hard-headed Woman; T-R-0-U-B-L-E; Dixieland Rock* Side 2: *Don't Ask Me Why; Lover Doll; Crawfish; Young Dreams; Steadfast, Loyal and True; New Orleans*

7.   **LPM-1951** (November 1958) *Elvis' Christmas Album* (re-issue with new cover and prefix).

8.   **LPM-1990** (February 1959) *For LP Fans Only* Side 1: *That's All Right; Laudy, Miss Claudy; Mystery Train; Playing for Keeps; Poor Boy* Side 2: *My Baby Left Me, I Was the One; Shake, Rattle and Roll; I'm Left, You're Right, She's Gone; You're a Heartbreaker*

9.   **LPM-2011** (September 1959) *A Date with Elvis* Side 1: *Blue Moon of Kentucky; Young and Beautiful; Baby, I Don't Care; Milkcow Blues Boogie; Baby, Let's Play House* Side 2: *Good Rockin' Tonight; Is It So Strange; We're Gonna Move; I Want to Be Free; I Forgot to Remember to Forget*

10.   **LPM-2075** (December 1959) *50,000,000 Elvis Fans Can't Be Wrong* Side 1: *I Need Your Love Tonight; Don't; Wear My Ring Around Your Neck; My Wish Came True; I Got Stung* Side 2: *One Night; A Big Hunk o'Love; I Beg of You; A

Fool Such as I; Doncha' Think It's Time

11. **LSP/LPM-2231** (April 1960) *Elvis Is Back!* Side 1: *Make Me Know It; Fever; The Girl of My Best Friend; I Will Be Home Again; Dirty, Dirty Feeling; Thrill of Your Love* Side 2: *Soldier Boy; Such a Night; It Feels So Right; The Girl Next Door (Went Awalking); Like a Baby; Reconsider, Baby*

12. **LSP/LPM-2256** (October 1960) *G.I. Blues* Side 1: *Tonight Is So Right for Love; What's She Really Like; Frankfort Special; Wooden Heart; G.I. Blues* Side 2: *Pocketful of Rainbows; Shoppin' Around; Big Boots; Didja Ever; Blue Suede Shoes; Doin'the Best I Can*

13. **LSP/LPM-2328** (December 1960) *His Hand in Mine* Side 1: *His Hand in Mine; I'm Gonna Walk Dem Golden Stairs; In My Father's House; Milky White Way; Known Only to Him; I Believe in the Man in the Sky* Side 2: *Joshua Fit the Battle; Jesus Knows Just What I Need; Swing Down, Sweet Chariot; Mansion over the Hilltop; If We Never Meet Again; Working on the Building*

14. **LSP/LPM-2370** (June 1961) *Something for Everybody* Side 1: *There's Always Me; Give Me the Right; It's a Sin; Sentimental Me; Starting Today; Gently* Side 2: *I'm Comin' Home; In Your Arms; Put the Blame on Me; Judy; I Want You with Me; I Slipped, I Stumbled, I Fell*

15. **LSP/LPM-2426** (October 1961) *Blue Hawaii* Side 1: *Blue Hawaii; Almost True; Aloha Oe; No More; Can't Help Falling in Love; Rock-a-Hula Baby; Moonlight Swim* Side 2: *Ku-u-i-po; Ito Eats; Slicin' Sand; Hawaiian Sunset; Beach Boy Blues; Island of Love; Hawaiian Wedding Song*

16. **LSP/LPM-2523** (June 1962) *Pot Luck* Side 1: *Kiss Me Quick; Just for Old Time Sake; Gonna Get Back Home Somehow; (Such an) Easy Question: Steppin' Out of Line; I'm Yours* Side 2: *Something Blue; Suspicion; I Feel That I've Known You Forever; Night Rider; Fountain of Love; That's Someone You Never Forget*

17. **LSP/LPM-2621** (November 1962) *Girls! Girls! Girls!* Side 1: *Girls! Girls! Girls!; I Don't Wanna Be Tied; Where Do You Come From; I Don't Want To; We'll Be Together; A Boy Like Me, a Girl Like You; Earth Boy* Side 2: *Return to Sender; Because of Love; Thanks to the Rolling Sea; Song of the Shrimp; The Walls Have Ears; We're Comin' In Loaded*

18. **LSP/LPM-2697** (April 1963) *It Happened at the World's Fair* Side 1: *Beyond the Bend; Relax; Take Me to the Fair; They Remind Me Too Much of You; One Broken Heart for Sale* Side 2: *I'm Falling in Love Tonight; Cotton Candy Land; A World of Our Own; How Would You Like to Be; Happy Ending*

19. **LSP/LPM-2765** (September 1963) *Elvis' Golden Records, Volume III* Side 1: *It's Now or Never; Stuck on You; Fame and Fortune; I Gotta Know; Surrender; I Feel So Bad* Side 2: *Are You Lonesome Tonight?; His Latest Flame; Little Sister; Good Luck Charm; Anything That's Part of You; She's Not You*

20. **LSP/LPM-2756** (December 1963) *Fun in Acapulco* Side 1: *Fun in Acapulco; Vino, Dinero y Amor; Mexico; El Toro; Marguerite; The Bullfighter Was a Lady; No Room to Rhumba in a Sports Car* Side 2: *I Think I'm Gonna Like It Here; Bossa Nova Baby; You Can't Say No in Acapulco; Guadalajara; Love Me Tonight; Slowly but Surely*

21. **LSP/LPM-2894** (March 1964) *Kissin' Cousins* Side 1: *Kissin' Cousins; Smokey Mountain Boy; There's Gold in the Mountains; One Boy, Two Little Girls; Catchin' On Fast; Tender Feeling* Side 2: *Anyone; Barefoot Ballad; Once Is Enough; Kissin' Cousins; Echoes of Love: Long Lonely Highway*

22. **LSP/LPM-2999** (October 1964) *Roustabout* Side 1: *Roustabout; Little Egypt; Poison Ivy League; Hard Knocks; It's a Wonderful World; Big Love, Big Heartache* Side 2: *One-track Heart; It's Carnival Time; Carny Town; There's a Brand New Day on the Horizon; Wheels on My Heels*

Elvis Spotter circa 1956

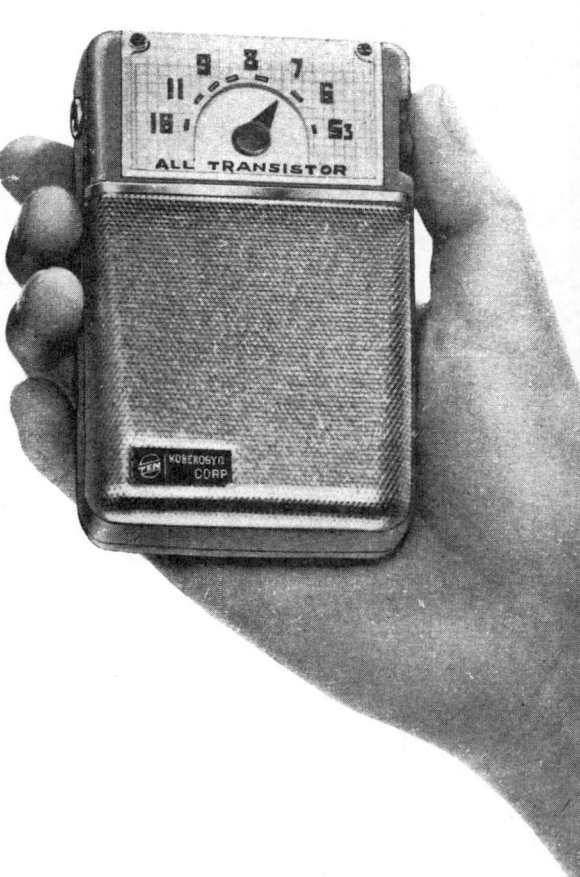

DOUBLE THE FEE? On hearing that MGM wanted his star, Elvis Presley, to play two roles in a new movie, Kissin' Cousins, manager Colonel Tom Parker retorted, "That's just fine. But does he get double the salary?"

— News report

23. **LSP/LPM-3338** (April 1965) *Girl Happy* Side 1: *Girl Happy; Spring Fever; Fort Lauderdale Chamber of Commerce; Startin' Tonight; Wolf Call; Do Not Disturb* Side 2: *Cross My Heart and Hope to Die; The Meanest Girl in Town; Do the Clam; Puppet on a String; I've Got to Find My Baby; You'll Be Gone*

24. **LSP/LPM-3450** (July 1965) *Elvis for Everyone* Side 1: *Your Cheatin' Heart; Summer Kisses, Winter Tears; Finders Keepers, Losers Weepers; In My Way; Tomorrow Night; Memphis, Tennessee* Side 2: *For the Millionth and the Last Time; Forget Me Never; Sound Advice; Santa Lucia; I Met Her Today; When It Rains, It Really Pours*

25. **LSP/LPM-3468** (October 1965) *Harum Scarum* Side 1: *Harum Holiday; My Desert Serenade; Go East, Young Man; Mirage; Kismet; Shake That Tambourine* Side 2: *Hey, Little Girl; Golden Coins; So Close, Yet So Far; Animal Instinct; Wisdom of the Ages*

26. **LSP/LPM-3553** (April 1966) *Frankie and Johnny* Side 1: *Frankie and Johnny; Come Along; Petunia, the Gardener's Daughter; Chesay; What Every Woman Lives For; Look Out, Broadway* Side 2: *Beginner's Luck; Down by the Riverside/When the Saints Go Marching In; Shout It Out; Hard Luck; Please Don't Stop Loving Me; Everybody Come Aboard*

27. **LSP/LPM-3643** (June 1966) *Paradise, Hawaiian Style* Side 1: *Paradise, Hawaiian Style; Queenie Wahine's Papaya; Scratch My Back, Drums of the Islands; Datin'* Side 2: *A Dog's Life, House of Sand; Stop Where You Are; This Is My Heaven; Sand Castles*

28. **LSP/LPM-3702** (October 1966) *Spinout* Side 1: *Stop, Look and Listen; Adam and Evil; All That I Am; Never Say Yes; Am I Ready; Beach Shack* Side 2: *Spinout; Smorgasbord; I'll Be Back; Tomorrow Is a Long Time, Down in the Alley; I'll Remember You*

29. **LSP/LPM-3758** (March 1967) *How Great Thou Art* Side 1: *How Great Thou Art; In the Garden; Somebody Bigger Than You and I; Farther Along; Stand by Me; Without Him* Side 2: *So High; Where Could I Go But to the Lord; By and By; If the Lord Wasn't Walking by My Side; Run On; Where No One Stands Alone; Crying in the Chapel*

30. **LSP/LPM-3787** (June 1967) *Double Trouble* Side 1: *Double Trouble; Baby, if You'll Give Me All Of Your Love; Could I Fall in Love; Long-legged Girl; City by Night; Old MacDonald* Side 2: *I Love Only One Girl; There Is So Much World to See, It Won't Be Long; Never Ending; Blue River; What Now, What Next, Where To*

31. **LSP/LPM-3893** (November 1967) *Clambake* Side 1: *Guitar Man; Clambake; Who Needs Money; A House That Has Everything; Confidence; Hey, Hey, Hey* Side 2: *You Don't Know Me; The Girl I Never Loved; How Can You Lose What You Never Had; Big Boss Man; Singing Tree; Just Call Me Lonesome*

32. **LSP/LPM-3921** (February 1968) *Elvis' Gold Records, Volume IV* Side 1: *Love Letters; Witchcraft; It Hurts Me; What'd I Say; Please Don't Drag That String Around; Indescribably Blue* Side 2: *(You're the) Devil in Disguise; Lonely Man; A Mess of Blues; Ask Me; Ain't That Loving You, Baby; Just Tell Her Jim Said Hello*

33. **LSP-3989** (June 1968) *Speedway* Side 1: *Speedway; There Ain't Nothing Like a Song; Your Time Hasn't Come Yet, Baby; Who Are You?; He's Your Uncle, Not Your Dad; Let Yourself Go* Side 2: *Your Groovy Self; Five Sleepy Heads; Western Union; Mine; Goin' Home; Suppose*

34. **LPM-4088** (December 1968) *Elvis – TV Special* Side 1: *Trouble/Guitar Man; Lawdy, Miss Clawdy/Baby, What You Want Me to Do; Heartbreak Hotel, Hound Dog; All Shook Up/Can't Help Falling in Love; Jailhouse Rock /(Dialogue); Love Me Tender* Side 2: *(Dialogue); Where Could I Go But to the Lord; Up Above My Head/Saved; Blue Christmas/One Night; Memories; Medley: Nothingville/Big*

Boss Man/Guitar Man/Little Egypt; T-R-O-U-B-L-E; Guitar Man; If I Can Dream

35. LSP-4155 (June 1969) *From Elvis in Memphis* Side 1: *Wearin' That Loved-on Look; Only the Strong Survive; I'll Hold You in My Heart; Long Black Limousine; It Keeps Right on A-hurtin'; I'm Movin' On* Side 2: *Power Of My Love; Gentle on My Mind; After Loving You; True Love Travels on a Gravel Road; Any Day Now; In the Ghetto*

36. LSP-6020 (November 1969) *From Memphis to Vegas/From Vegas to Memphis* Side 1: *Blue Suede Shoes; Johnny B. Goode; All Shook Up; Are You Lonesome Tonight?; Hound Dog; I Can't Stop Loving You; My Babe* Side 2: *Mystery Train/Tiger Man; Words; In the Ghetto; Suspicious Minds; Can't Help Falling in Love* Side 3: *Inherit the Wind; This Is the Story; Stranger in My Own Home Town; A Little Bit of Green; And the Grass Won't Pay No Mind* Side 4: *Do You Know Who I Am; From a Jack to a King; The Fair's Moving On; You'll Think of Me; Without Love (There Is Nothing)*

37. LSP-4428 (February 1970) *Elvis in Person* (features same tracks as live segments from LSP 6020, Sides 1 and 2).

38. LSP-4362 (June 1970) *On Stage, February, 1970* Side 1: *See See Rider; Release Me; Sweet Caroline; Runaway; The Wonder of You* Side 2: *Polk Salad Annie; Yesterday; Proud Mary; Walk a Mile in My Shoes, Let It Be Me*

39. LPM-6401 (August 1970) *Elvis: Worldwide 50 Gold Award Hits, Volume I* Side 1: *Heartbreak Hotel; I Was the One; I Want You, I Need You, I Love You; Don't Be Cruel; Hound Dog; Love Me Tender* Side 2: *Any Way You Want Me; Too Much; Playing for Keeps; (I'm) All Shook Up; That's When Your Heartaches Begin; Loving You* Side 3: *Teddy Bear; Jailhouse Rock; Treat Me Nice; I Beg of You; Don't; Wear My Ring Around Your Neck; Hard-headed Woman* Side 4: *I Got Stung; A Fool Such as I; A Big Hunk o'Love; Stuck on You; A Mess of Blues; It's Now or Never* Side 5: *I Gotta Know; Are You Lonesome Tonight?; Surrender; I Feel So Bad; Little Sister; Can't Help Falling in Love* Side 6: *Rock-a-hula Baby; Anything That's Part of You; Good Luck Charm; She's Not You; Return to Sender; Where Do You Come From; One Broken Heart for Sale* Side 7: *(You're the) Devil in Disguise; Bossa Nova Baby; Kissin' Cousins; Viva Las Vegas; Ain't That Loving You, Baby; Wooden Heart* Side 8: *Crying in the Chapel; If I Can Dream; In the Ghetto; Suspicious Minds; Don't Cry, Daddy; Kentucky Rain; Excerpts from Elvis Sails*

40. LSP-4429 (November 1970) *Back in Memphis* (features the studio tracks from LSP 6020, Sides 3 and 4).

41. LSP-4445 (December 1970) *That's the Way It Is* Side 1: *I just Can't Help Believin'; Twenty Days and Twenty Nights; How the Web Was Woven; Patch It Up; Mary in the Morning; You Don't Have to Say You Love Me* Side 2: *You've Lost That Lovin' Feelin'; I've Lost You; Just Pretend; Stranger in the Crowd; The Next Step Is Love; Bridge over Troubled Water*

42. LSP-4460 (January 1971) *Elvis Country* Side 1: *Snowbird; Tomorrow Never Comes; Little Cabin on the Hill; Whole Lotta Shakin' Goin' On; Funny How Time Slips Away; I Really Don't Want to Know* Side 2: *There Goes My Everything; It's Your Baby, You Rock It; The Fool; Faded Love; I Washed My Hands in Muddy Water; Make the World Go Away*

43. LSP-4530 (June 1971) *Love Letters from Elvis* Side 1: *Love Letters; When I'm Over You; If I Were You; Got My Mojo Working; Heart of Rome* Side 2: *Only Believe; This Is Our Dance; Cindy, Cindy; I'll Never Know; It Ain't No Big Thing; Life*

44. LPM-6402 (August 1971) *Elvis: The Other Sides; Worldwide Gold Award Hits, Volume II* Side 1: *Puppet on a String; Witchcraft; T-B-O-U-B-L-E; Poor Boy; I*

Want to Be Free; Doncha'Think It's Time; Young Dreams Side 2: The Next Step Is Love; You Don't Have to Say You Love Me, Paralyzed; My Wish Came True, When My Blue Moon Turns to Gold Again; Lonesome Cowboy Side 3: My Baby Left Me; It Hurts Me; I Need Your Love Tonight; Tell Me Why; Please Don't Drag That String Around; Young and Beautiful Side 4: Hot Dog; New Orleans; We're Gonna Move; Crawfish; King Creole; I Believe in the Man in the Sky, Dixieland Rock Side 5: The Wonder of You; They Remind Me Too Much of You; Mean Woman Blues; Lonely Man; Any Day Now; Don't Ask Me Why Side 6: His Latest Flame; I Really Don't Want to Know; Baby, I Don't Care; I've Lost You; Let Me; Love Me Side 7: Got a Lot o' Livin' to Do; Fame and Fortune; Rip It Up; There Goes My Everything; Lover Doll; One Night Side 8: Just Tell Her Jim Said Hello; Ask Me; Patch It Up; As Long As I Have You; You'll Think of Me; Wild in the Country

45. LSP-4579 (October 1971) *The Wonderful World of Christmas* Side 1: *O Come, All Ye Faithful; The First Noel; On a Snowy Christmas Night; Winter Wonderland; The Wonderful World of Christmas; It Won't Seem Like Christmas (Without You)* Side 2: *I'll Be Home on Christmas Day; If I Get Home on Christmas Day; Holly Leaves and Christmas Trees; Merry Christmas, Baby; Silver Bells*

46. LSP-4671 (January 1972) *Elvis Now* Side 1: *Help Me Make It Through the Night; Miracle of the Rosary; Hey, Jude; Put Your Hand in the Hand; Until It's Time for You to Go* Side 2: *We Can Make the Morning; Early Mornin'Rain; Sylvia; Fools Rush In; I Was Born About 10,000 Years Ago*

47. LSP-4690 (April 1972) *He Touched Me* Side 1: *He Touched Me; I've Got Confidence; Amazing Grace; Seeing Is Believing; He Is My Everything; Bosom of Abraham* Side 2: *An Evening Prayer; Lead Me, Guide Me; There Is No God But God; A Thing Called Love; I John; Reach Out to Jesus*

48. LSP-4776 (June 1972) *Elvis As Recorded at Madison Square Garden* Side 1: *Also Sprach Zarathustra; That's All Right; Proud Mary; Never Been to Spain; You Don't Have to Say You Love Me; You've Lost That Lovin' Feelin'; Polk Salad Annie; Love Me; All Shook Up; Heartbreak Hotel; Medley: Teddy Bear/Don't Be Cruel/Love Me Tender* Side 2: *The Impossible Dream; Introductions by Elvis; Hound Dog; Suspicious Minds; For the Good Times; American Trilogy; Funny How Time Slips Away; I Can't Stop Loving You; Can't Help Falling in Love*

49. VPX-6089 (February 1973) *Elvis: Aloha from Hawaii* Side 1: *Also Sprach Zarathustra; See See Rider; Burning Love; Something; Lord, This Time You Gave Me a Mountain; Steamroller Blues* Side 2: *My Way; Love Me; Johnny B. Goode; It's Over; Blue Suede Shoes; I'm So Lonesome I Could Cry; I Can't Stop Loving You; Hound Dog* Side 3: *What Now, My Love; Fever; Welcome to My World; Suspicious Minds; Introductions by Elvis* Side 4: *I'll Remember You; Medley: Long Tall Sally/A Whole Lotta Shakin' Goin' On; American Trilogy; A Big Hunk o' Love; Can't Help Falling in Love*

50. APL-0283 (June 1973) *Elvis* Side 1: *Fool; Where Do I Go from Here; Love Me, Love the Life I Lead; It's Still Here; It's Impossible* Side 2: *For Lovin' Me; Padre; I'll Take You Home Again, Kathleen; I Will Be True; Don't Think Twice, It's All Right*

51. APL-0388 (October 1973) *Raised on Rock* Side 1: *Raised on Rock; Are You Sincere; Find Out What's Happening; I Miss You; Girl of Mine* Side 2: *For Ol' Times Sake; If You Don't Come Back; Just a Little Bit; Sweet Angeline; Three Corn Patches*

52. CPL-0341 (January 1974) *A Legendary Performer, Volume I* Side 1: *That's All Right; I Love You Because; Heartbreak Hotel; Don't Be Cruel; Love Me; Tryin' to Get to You* Side 2: *Love Me Tender; Peace in the Valley; A Fool Such as I; Tonight's All Right for Love; Are You Lonesome Tonight?; Can't Help Falling in Love*

53. **CPL-0475** (March 1974) *Good Times* Side 1: *Take Good Care of Her; Loving Arms; I Got a Feelin' in My Body; If That Isn't Love; She Wears My Ring* Side 2: *I've Got a Thing About You, Baby; My Boy; Spanish Eyes; Talk About the Good Times; Goodtime Charlie's Got the Blues*

54. **CPL-0606** (June 1974) *Elvis: Recorded Live on Stage in Memphis* Side 1: *See See Rider; I Got a Woman; Love Me; Tryin' to Get to You; Medley: Long Tall Sally/Whole Lotta Shakin' Goin' On/Your Mama Won't Dance/Flip, Flop and Fly/Jailhouse Rock/Hound Dog; Why Me, Lord; How Great Thou Art* Side 2: *Medley: Blueberry Hill/I Can't Stop Loving You; Help Me; An American Trilogy, Let Me Be There; My Baby Left Me; Lawdy, Miss Clawdy, Can't Help Falling in Love; Closing vamp*

55. **CPM-0818** (October 1974) *Having Fun with Elvis on Stage*

56. **APL-0873** (January 1975) *Promised Land* Side 1: *Promised Land; There's a Honky Tonk Angel; Help Me; Mr. Songman; Love Song of the Year* Side 2: *It's Midnight; Your Love's Been a Long Time Coming; If You Talk in Your Sleep; Thinking About You; You Asked Me To*

57. **ANL-0971** (March 1975) *Pure Gold* Side 1: *Kentucky Rain; Fever; It's Impossible; Jailhouse Rock; Don't Be Cruel* Side 2: *I Got a Woman; All Shook Up; Loving You; In the Ghetto; Love Me Tender*

58. **APL-1039** (June 1975) *Today* Side 1: *T-R-O-U-B-L-E; And I Love You So; Susan When She Tried; Woman Without Love; Shake a Hand* Side 2: *Pieces of My Life; Fairytale; I Can Help; Banging It Back; Green, Green Grass of Home*

59. **CPL-1349** (January 1976) *A Legendary Performer, Volume II* Side 1: *Harbor Lights; Interview with Elvis; I Want You, I Need You, I Love You; Blue Suede Shoes; Blue Christmas; Jailhouse Rock; It's Now or Never* Side 2: *A Cane and a High Starched Collar; Presentation of Awards to Elvis; Blue Hawaii; Such a Night; Baby, What You Want Me to Do; How Great Thou Art; If I Can Dream*

60. **ANL-1319** (March 1976) *His Hand in Mine* (Reissue by RCA on Pure Gold series: same selections as LSP/LPM 2328).

61. **APM-1675** (March 1976) *The Sun Sessions* Side 1: *That's All Right; Blue Moon of Kentucky; I Don't Care if the Sun Don't Shine; Good Rockin' Tonight; Milkcow Blues Boogie; You're a Heartbreaker; I'm Left, You're Right, She's Gone; Baby, Let's Play House* Side 2: *Mystery Train; I Forgot to Remember to Forget; I'll Never Let You Go; I Love You Because; Tryin' to Get to You; Blue Moon; Just Because; I Love You Because*

62. **APL-1506** (May 1976) *From Elvis Presley Boulevard, Memphis, Tennessee* Side 1: *Hurt; Never Again; Blue Eyes Crying in the Rain; Danny Boy; The Last Farewell* Side 2: *For the Heart; Bitter They Are, Harder They Fall; Solitaire; Love Coming Down; I'll Never Fall in Love Again*

63. **ANL-1936** (November 1976) *The Wonderful World of Christmas* (Reissue by RCA on Pure Gold Series: same selections as LSP-4579).

64. **APL-2274** (March 1977) *Welcome to My World* Side 1: *Welcome to My World (live); Help Me Make It Through the Night; Release Me (and Let Me Love Again) (live); I Really Don't Want to Know; For the Good Times (live)* Side 2: *Make the World Go Away (live); Gentle on My Mind; I'm So Lonesome I Could Cry (live); Your Cheatin' Heart; I Can't Stop Loving You (live)*

65. **AFL-2428** (June 1977) *MOODY BLUE* Side 1: *Unchained Melody; If You Love Me (Let Me Know); Little Darlin'; He'll Have to Go; Let Me Be There* Side 2: *Way Down; Pledging My Love; Moody Blue; She Thinks I Still Care; It's Easy for You*

"Singers come and go, but if you're a good actor you can last a long time."
— Elvis

ELVIS SPOTTER'S QUIZ - ANSWERS

1. Priscilla Beaulieu.
2. Fear of the sight of blood.
3. Thirty-one plus two documentaries.
4. *Loving You.*
5. Enrico Caruso.
6. Honey.
7. 2001.
8. Taking Care of Business.
9. A pink Cadillac.
10. Getlow.
11. Hawaiian shirt and a baseball cap.
12. 22.
13. East Germany.
14. Lisa Marie.
15. Memphis.
16. *Kissin' Cousins.*
17. "It's All Right Mama".
18. Hilton.
19. Colonel Tom Parker.
20. 1958.
21. Lincoln Zephyr coupe.
22. *Elvis Is Back!*
23. Marvel.
24. *Roustabout.*
25. *Heartbreak Hotel.*
26. US.
27. Crown Electric.
28. He stuttered.
29. Jerry Lee Lewis.
30. James Dean.
31. 1968.
32. Chickens.
33. *Harum Scarum.*
34. $100,000.
35. *Girls, Girls, Girls; Girl Happy; The Trouble With Girls.*
36. 3764 Elvis Presley Boulevard (formerly Highway 51 South), Memphis, Tennessee.
37. Diet soft drinks.
38. Fear of the ocean.
39. Go-cart.
40. 6 lbs, 15 ounces.
41. Aladdin Hotel.
42. Two.
43. *Don't Be Cruel.*
44. Blue/Hazel.
45. A sewing-machine operator.
46. A Corvair car.
47. *Love Me Tender.*
48. "She Was The Sunshine Of Our Home".
49. Eight-eighty Echo Papa.
50. Danielle Riley Keough.
51. His mother and Jesus.
52. *Love Me Tender.*
53. *Eskimo Pies, Nutty Buddys, Fudgesicles* and *Dreamsickles.*
54. Colgate.
55. 32.
56. *Charro.*
57. Harley Davidson.
58. 11D in US sizing.
59. Capricorn.
60. *Flaming Star.*
61. Gold and blue.
62. *Dream.*
63. Mary Tyler Moore.
64. Corinthians I:13.
65. Satnin'.
66. Karate.
67. 1953.
68. Rising Sun.
69. *Paradise.*
70. "comfort".
71. 1967.
72. Hal Wallis.
73. Hermann Goering.
74. Ginger Alden.
75. Football.
76. *Loving You.*
77. Monopoly.
78. Domino.
79. John Baron.
80. Jon Burrows.
81. *Loving You.*
82. Louisiana.
83. Sergeant.
84. *Blue Moon of Kentucky.*
85. Nancy Sinatra.
86. Fire eyes.
87. He delivered him.
88. Brigitte Bardot.
89. *Crazy.*
90. Eddie Murphy.
91. Cilla.
92. *Flaming Star.*
93. A face-lift.
94. University of Tennessee at Knoxville.
95. Jeep driver.
96. Derringer.
97. L.C. Humes High School.
98. Gladys Love Smith.
99. "Sooties" (from "footies").
100. Betty McMann.

ELVIS REWARD - TERMS AND CONDITIONS

The London *Sun* newspaper back in 1989 offered ONE MILLION POUNDS for anyone who could bring Elvis to the newspaper's offices alive. Obviously, that was not enough to tempt the King to reveal himself - or enough incentive for spotters.

So the publishers of THE ELVIS SPOTTER'S GUIDE, listed on Page 6 of this book, have decided to double the reward to the amount shown on the reward posted on Page 2.

The reward will be payable in full only to the person who presents Elvis Aaron Presley, US Army serial number US53310761, in person to the Publishers of THE ELVIS SPOTTER'S GUIDE at their offices. To qualify for the reward, the person you present to the Publishers as being Elvis Aaron Presley, US Army serial number US53310761, must meet ALL of the following terms and conditions listed below to the full and complete satisfaction of the Publishers:

1. The person purporting to be Elvis Aaron Presley must be alive and be able and willing to tell in detail how he "died" at Graceland, 3764 Elvis Presley Boulevard, Memphis, Tennessee, on 16 August 1977 and every detail of his life since that date. He must also be able to sing and dance to rock-'n-roll music, wearing blue suede shoes if required by the Publishers of THE ELVIS SPOTTER'S GUIDE.

2. The fingerprints of the person purporting to be Elvis Aaron Presley must match that of Elvis Aaron Presley, US Army serial number US53310761, on file with the U.S. Government, to the satisfaction of fingerprint experts retained by and at the sole discretion of the Publishers of THE ELVIS SPOTTER'S GUIDE.

3. The teeth of the person purporting to be Elvis Aaron Presley must match dental records of Elvis Aaron Presley, US Army serial number US53310761, held on file by the dentist who attended to the said Elvis Aaron Presley, to the satisfaction of dental experts retained by and at the sole discretion of the Publishers of THE ELVIS SPOTTER'S GUIDE.

4. The person purporting to be Elvis Aaron Presley must be able to sing, with musical accompaniment but without written copies of the lyrics, any of the songs recorded by the said Elvis Aaron Presley, US Army serial number US53310761, on the RCA and Sun Records labels and listed in THE ELVIS SPOTTER'S GUIDE, to the satisfaction of a panel of Elvis Presley music experts, such panel to be appointed by and at the sole discretion of the Publishers of THE ELVIS SPOTTER'S GUIDE.

5. The person purporting to be Elvis Aaron Presley must match all the physical characteristics listed in THE ELVIS READY RECKONER in THE ELVIS SPOTTER'S GUIDE, to the satisfaction of a panel of medical experts, such panel to be appointed by and at the sole discretion of the Publishers of THE ELVIS SPOTTER'S GUIDE.

6. The person purporting to be Elvis Aaron Presley must sign a world-wide exclusive contract with the Publishers of THE ELVIS SPOTTER'S GUIDE for the publication of his life story since 16 August 1977. Any interviews or comments about his life since that date to any other media outlet whatsoever will make the person presenting the person purporting to be Elvis Aaron Presley ineligible for the reward or for any payment whatsoever from the Publishers of THE ELVIS SPOTTER'S GUIDE.

7. The person purporting to be Elvis Aaron Presley must sign a world-wide exclusive contract with the Publishers of THE ELVIS SPOTTER'S GUIDE for the publication of all photographs/film/video recordings to be taken of him for a period of 20 years after the time he first presents himself to the Publishers of THE ELVIS SPOTTER'S GUIDE.

The Publishers of THE ELVIS SPOTTER'S GUIDE will not be liable for any payments to anyone other than the amount of the reward listed on page 2 and subject to the terms and conditions set out above.

All expenses incurred for tests as described above and for any other tests ordered by the Publishers of THE ELVIS SPOTTER'S GUIDE at their sole discretion to prove or disprove the identity of the person purporting to be Elvis Aaron Presley must be borne in full by the person making the claim and no refund will be made under any circumstances whatsoever.